GEORGE WASHINGTON

THE AMERICAN HEROES SERIES

Amelia Earhart: The Sky's No Limit by Lori Van Pelt
Chief Joseph: Guardian of the People by Candy Moulton
John Muir: Magnificent Tramp by Rod Miller
Mary Edwards Walker: Above and Beyond by Dale L. Walker
David Crockett: Hero of the Common Man
by William Groneman III
George Washington: First in War, First in Peace
by James A. Crutchfield

Dale L. Walker, General Editor

Also by James A. Crutchfield

The Way West: True Stories of the American Frontier, editor
The Grand Adventure: A Year-by-Year History of Virginia
Legends of the Wild West, co-author with Bill O'Neal
and Dale L. Walker
Opryland Hotel: Nashville; The Story of an American Classic
Mountain Men of the American West
America's Yesteryears
Eyewitness to American History
The Santa Fe Trail
Tragedy at Taos: The Revolt of 1847
It Happened in Georgia
It Happened in Texas
It Happened in New Mexico
It Happened in Washington
It Happened in Oregon
It Happened in Arizona
It Happened in Colorado
It Happened in Montana
Tennesseans at War
The Natchez Trace: A Pictorial History

GEORGE WASHINGTON

First in War, First in Peace

JAMES A. CRUTCHFIELD

A Tom Doherty Associates Book
New York

A Forge Book
Published by Tom Doherty Associates, LLC
175 Fifth Avenue
New York, NY 10010

www.tor.com

Forge® is a registered trademark of
Tom Doherty Associates, LLC.

Library of Congress Cataloging-in-Publication Data

Crutchfield, James Andrew, 1938–
    George Washington : first in war, first in peace / James A. Crutchfield.
        p. cm. — (The American heroes series)
    "A Tom Doherty Associates book."
    Includes bibliographical references (p. 223) and index (p. 229).
    ISBN 0-765-31069-4
    EAN 978-0-765-31069-9
    1. Washington, George, 1732–1799. 2. Presidents—United States—Biography.
3. Generals—United States—Biography. 4. Heroes—United States—Biography.
I. Title. II. American heroes series (New York, N.Y.)

E312.C87 2005
973.4'1'092—dc22
[B]
                                                                    2005047889

First Edition: November 2005

PRINTED IN THE UNITED STATES OF AMERICA

0 9 8 7 6 5 4 3 2 1

To Regena,
My life partner, soul mate, wife, and best friend

First in war, first in peace, and first in the hearts of his country-men, he was second to none in humble and enduring scenes of private life. Pious, just, humane, temperate, and sincere; uniform, dignified, and commanding. . . . Such was the man for whom our nation mourns.

Henry "Light-Horse Harry" Lee
December 26, 1799

Contents

Foreword by Dale L. Walker 17

1. "I Can Read Three or Four Pages Sometimes
Without Missing a Word" 25

GEORGE WASHINGTON AND THE CHERRY TREE **31**

2. "A Charming Field for an Encounter" 33

3. "I Heard the Bullets Whistle. . . . There Is Something
Charming in the Sound" 40

4. "I Would Be a Willing Offering
to Savage Fury" 47

Contents

5. "Enquire . . . in the Neighborhood, & Get Some Egg's and Chickens" 55

6. "Some Thing Shou'd Be Done to . . . Maintain . . . Liberty" 63

7. "I Do Not Think My-Self Equal to the Command I Am Honored With" 72

8. "We Are Determined to Shake Off All Connexions with a State So Unjust" 80

MARTHA WASHINGTON 85

9. "Good God! Have I Got Such Troops as These?" 87

10. "I Am Now Convinced . . . This Army Must . . . Starve, Dissolve, or Disperse" 95

11. "My Temper Leads Me to Peace and Harmony with All Men" 102

12. "Unless Congress Speaks in a More Decisive Tone . . . Our Cause Is Lost" 109

13. "A Reduction of the British Army . . . Is Most Happily Effected" 116

BENEDICT ARNOLD 123

Contents

14. "With a Heart Full of . . . Gratitude, I Now Take
Leave of You" 126

15. "I Am at Length Become a Private Citizen . . .
on the Banks of the Patowmac" 134

GEORGE WASHINGTON ON SLAVERY 140

16. "If Nothing Had Been Agreed On . . . Anarchy Would
Soon Have Ensued" 143

17. "I Entered upon My Administration . . . with
the Best Intentions" 152

18. "Frequent Incursions Have Been Made
on Our Frontier" 160

19. "Differences in Political Opinions Are . . .
Unavoidable" 168

20. "We . . . Cannot Deny . . . the Right Whereon Our
Own Government Is Founded" 176

21. "A Mission Like This . . . Will Announce . . . Solicitude
for Friendly Adjustment" 183

22. "I Have, with Good Intentions, Contributed Towards
the . . . Government" 190

Contents

THE VIRGINIA DYNASTY 196

23. "Everything We Hold Dear and Sacred [Is] . . .
    Seriously Threatened" 200

24. "Let Me Go Off Quietly; I Cannot Last Long" 207

Epilogue 217

Acknowledgments and Sources 223

Index 229

Foreword

A year after the Father of Our Country died, Mason Locke Weems of Maryland, an Anglican clergyman, published *The Life and Memorable Actions of George Washington*. His book was immensely popular, attributing to Washington a faultless life of supernatural wisdom and honesty, the saintly portrait receiving a final brushstroke in the fifth edition (1806) in which Parson Weems invented the great cherry-tree-chopping, "I cannot tell a lie" tale.

Thus began the process of adding gilt to an already golden story, the result of which, historian Daniel Boorstin states, is that Washington "attained a stature in death that he never had in life. A deification which in European history might have required centuries was accomplished here in decades."

Thomas Jefferson, Washington's secretary of state, said of his fellow Virginian, "He was, indeed, in every sense of the word, a wise, a good, and a great man."

Benjamin Franklin characterized him as "one of the greatest captains of the age."

The marquis de Lafayette wrote to his wife, "This friendship [with Washington] makes me as happy as I could possibly be away from you."

In his "Funeral Oration Upon George Washington," delivered December 26, 1799, before the houses of Congress, General Henry "Light-Horse Harry" Lee, the Revolutionary War commander and father of Robert E. Lee, summed up national sentiments with the words "First in war, first in peace, and first in the hearts of his countrymen."

Of course, not all of his contemporaries shared such sentiments during or after Washington's life. Tom Paine, in a French prison for seditious activity and embittered by Washington's neutrality in his case, said the president was "treacherous in private friendship," "a hyprocrite in public life," and "unprincipled." The anti-Federalist press excoriated him as "the scourge and misfortune of our country" and accused him of stealing from the treasury and being an inept general.

Even his best modern biographer, Douglas Southall Freeman, in his seven-volume *George Washington: A Biography* (1958), said the first president had "an ambition for wealth," made mistakes in his battles, was often insensitive to others, intolerant of political opposition, thin-skinned, and given to melancholy.

But aside from such divided opinion, natural in assessing so great a man, one of Washington's captivating characteristics is that, despite the immensity of research on him and the multivolume biographies, he remains the most baffling of the Founding Fathers. Nathaniel Hawthorne described him with an enigma: "He had no nakedness, but was born with his clothes on, and his hair powdered, and made a stately bow on his first appearance into the world." John Bach McMaster, biographer of Daniel Webster and author of a massive history of the United States, called Washington "an unknown man," and the Harvard historian Edward P. Channing said of him, "No more elusive personality exists in history."

Among the many works he consulted in writing this book, James A. Crutchfield was particularly impressed by *George Washington: The Image and the Man* (1926) by W. E. Woodward, biographer of Tom Paine and Lafayette. "One of the valuable statements Woodward made," Crutchfield says, "is that the key to understanding Washington is to remember him not as the flawless hero of our national beginnings but as 'the American common denominator, the average man deified and raised to the nth power.' This observation is important in my interpretation."

Crutchfield, author of many books on American history, says that in many ways Washington was an ordinary man thrust into extraordinary circumstances: "Unlike most of his peers, he began his career without the benefit of a university education, yet over the years elevated himself from relative anonymity as a surveyor and minor landowner to lead the thirteen American colonies through five years of grueling war to independence from British rule."

After his first great victories at Trenton (December 26, 1776) and Princeton (January 3, 1777), Washington was elevated to the role of national hero, so revered by the end of the war that,

Crutchfield says, "Some of his generals urged him to install himself as king over the loosely confederated union—an idea he looked upon with 'abhorrence,' calling the very thought 'painful.' Nor would he consider standing for a third term as president. He knew he had done what he could and that others needed to step forward. He meant what he wrote in his Farewell Address, 'I anticipate with pleasing anticipation that retreat, in which I promise myself to realize, without alloy. . . .' Among his common man attributes was a keen common sense."

Even so, as this book makes clear, Washington's commonness could be misleading. He was reticent, not much of a reader beyond the Bible and Alexander Pope's works, nor was he an eloquent speaker or easy conversationalist, but he possessed a quick mind, an eagerness to learn, and had what many said was an "uncommonly majestic and commanding presence." These attributes ensured his comfort in any company, from geniuses like his secretary of state, Thomas Jefferson, to aristocrats like the marquis de Lafayette (perhaps his closest confidant during the war), foreign dignitaries, and common soldiers.

Crutchfield's treatment of Washington the soldier, from his service as militia officer in the French and Indian War through his command of the Continental Army, is evenhanded. With no schooling or experience in the "art of war," as had such formidable contemporaries as Napoleon and the duke of Wellington, the Virginian was never a great strategist or tactician. Instead, he grew along with his responsibilities, learned from his mistakes, and had as integral to his character the patience and doggedness required for victory. He held his ragtag army together against all odds, sought battle at Long Island, Princeton, Brandywine, and

Yorktown, but was not afraid to withdraw from the field when necessary, to regroup and fight another day.

Above all, he had foresight—the ability to see that there would be a time of peace after a time of revolution and to ponder the problems of the nation in larger terms than the day's battle.

"Later, Washington's ability to see the 'bigger picture' served him well," the author says. "He would say that 'Government is not reason; it is not eloquence; it is force! Like fire, it is a dangerous servant and a fearful master.' Out of this belief he provided the clear-headed guidance to steer the proceedings of the Constitutional Convention, and twice serve as president, to assure that the new United States would develop the sound foundations required to thrust itself upon the world stage."

"The life of the Husbandman of all others is the most delectable," Washington wrote. "It is honorable. It is amusing and, with judicious management, it is profitable." And so, after eight years in war and eight as president, in 1797 he returned to his beloved Mount Vernon, his eight-thousand-acre plantation in Fairfax County, Virginia, above the Potomac with the woodlands of Maryland beyond the far shore—to his mansion with its grand pillared portico, brick walks, lawns, great trees, greenhouse, and gardens.

There, he read newspapers aloud to Martha, took daily walks, instructed his overseers, and died, on December 14, 1799, at the age of sixty-seven.

"There is something heroic about him even at the end of his

life," Crutchfield states. "His great work was done. He lived less than three years afterward but it was time enough to look back with satisfaction and forward with confidence that the nation would prosper. Parson Weems, who started all the unnecessary legendry about Washington, at least had it right when he said, 'Go thy way Old George. . . . We shall not look upon thy like again.'"

—DALE L. WALKER

GEORGE
WASHINGTON

"I Can Read Three or Four Pages Sometimes Without Missing a Word"

The large mantel clock in the dining room at Mount Vernon had just chimed eleven times when the three physicians once again entered George Washington's bedroom and looked despairingly upon his limp body. The doctors had been by the former president's side practically all day long, hoping against all odds that the sixty-seven-year-old warrior would show some signs of improvement. Now, as midnight rapidly approached, they glanced sadly at each other. There was no hope in their faces.

Martha Washington sat nearby, attended by a few house servants and her husband's private secretary, Tobias Lear. The room was cold. A mid-December snowstorm had swept down the Potomac River two days earlier and sent temperatures plummeting. Rushing about to keep the cavernous Mount Vernon as warm as possible, the servants heaped several additional blankets upon

Washington's listless body, leaving nothing exposed but his porcelainlike face.

Two of the physicians finally excused themselves and walked downstairs to await the inevitable. Dr. James Craik, a close associate whose friendship dated back to French and Indian War days, continued his vigil as Washington weakened. Shortly before midnight, he called Dr. Craik to his side and murmured, "My breath cannot last long." Sadly, Craik motioned to Martha that the end was near.

Within minutes Washington was dead, most likely from acute epiglottitis caused from a virulent bacterial infection. In his nearly seven decades on earth, he had, as military commander, led his new country to independence from Great Britain; later, as the first president, he orchestrated its great leap forward into the brotherhood of nations. He was indeed as his friend Henry "Light-Horse Harry" Lee declared a few days later in a resolution before Congress, "first in war, first in peace, and first in the hearts of his countrymen."

The Washington dynasty in America began with the arrival from England of John Washington, George's great-grandfather, around 1656. A successful tobacco farmer and public servant, he had, by the time of his death in 1677 at age forty-five, acquired a number of plantations and several thousand acres of Virginia land, including the site of Mount Vernon.

John Washington's son Lawrence was born in 1659 and, at age eighteen, following his father's death, inherited most of the estate. He pursued the life of a planter, served as sheriff of

Westmoreland County, and was elected to four terms in the House of Burgesses. He died in 1698 at age thirty-nine.

In 1694 Lawrence's second son, Augustine, was born on his grandfather's farm. Orphaned at the age of four, the boy was raised by his stepfather. In 1715 he married Jane Butler, by whom he eventually sired four children. Following in the footsteps of his grandfather and father, Augustine became prominent in the community. He served as a justice and as the sheriff of Westmoreland County, was commissioned a captain in the local militia, and owned forty-nine slaves, two iron furnaces, and property in three Virginia counties.

Jane Butler Washington died in 1729, leaving Augustine to care for two sons and a daughter (another child had died in infancy). Sixteen months later, he married Mary Ball from nearby Lancaster County. The couple's first child, George, arrived at ten o'clock on the morning of February 22, 1732 (or, according to the old-style calendar, February 11) at the family plantation in Westmoreland County, Virginia.

When George was three years old, his family relocated to Hunting Creek, the future Mount Vernon, another plantation owned by his father and located forty miles up the Potomac River from his birthplace. Three years later, the Washingtons moved again, this time to Ferry Farm, situated on the Rappahannock River near Fredericksburg. In addition to a modest six-room house and a paltry collection of household furnishings, George's father owned twenty slaves. It can be assumed that young Washington led a normal farm boy's life at Ferry Farm, running and romping in the woods, fishing, hunting, tormenting frogs and turtles in the nearby creek, playing soldier, and reading.

His hopes of attending school in England died with his father in 1743. His education at Ferry Farm was informal— and negligible—especially compared with the college degrees acquired by his future friends and associates (John Adams, Harvard; Thomas Jefferson, College of William and Mary; James Madison, Princeton). He learned quickly, however, and by age nine was bragging to his boyhood friend Richard Henry Lee, "I can read three or four pages sometimes without missing a word." During his quest for an education, the youngster also learned important maxims that would guide him for the rest of his life. Among his earliest known writings is a list of "The Rules of Civility and Decent Behavior in Company and Conversation," which he reproduced from an old text into his own copybook. Consisting of 110 proverbs, the list included such thoughts as "Keep your nails clean and short, also your hands and teeth clean, yet without showing any great concern for them," and "Use no reproachful language against any one; neither curse nor revile."

Over the next few years, George alternated between his mother's home at Ferry Farm, half brother Lawrence's Mount Vernon plantation, and half brother Augustine's farm, also on the Potomac. His favorite place was Mount Vernon, and in the absence of his father, he grew to rely heavily on the counsel and companionship of Lawrence, fourteen years older and an officer in the British army. His days at Mount Vernon were happy ones, and he rejoiced at hearing the stories of Lawrence's military exploits. On one occasion, he was even privileged to accompany

Lawrence to Barbados in search of a cure for the deadly tuberculosis that infected the elder Washington's lungs. The trip did nothing to help Lawrence, but during the journey George contracted a mild case of smallpox that provided him with lifetime immunity to the disease. Years later, during the awful winters of the Revolution, when large numbers of his soldiers died of the malady, he was spared.

Lawrence Washington's father-in-law and close neighbor at Mount Vernon was William Fairfax, the American agent for his cousin, Lord Thomas Fairfax of England. Lord Fairfax had been granted an enormous tract of land—at one time approaching five million acres—in the Shenandoah Valley and in the Northern Neck, the peninsula formed by the Potomac and Rappahannock Rivers and Chesapeake Bay. William Fairfax, the property's overseer, lived at Belvoir, a mansion that deeply impressed young Washington, who visited there often and became accustomed to—and appreciative of—the style of living of Virginia's wealthy class. He even visited with his lordship when the Englishman toured America.

Lord Fairfax took a liking to the youth and used his substantial influence to obtain a Royal Navy commission for him, but the boy's mother adamantly refused to allow him to leave home, especially after her brother opined that it was "better to put [George] apprentice to a Tinker." Still trying to help the lad, now age sixteen, his lordship gave him a job surveying his properties that lay beyond the distant Allegheny Mountains. Washington had always done well in mathematics and easily caught on to the surveyor's craft. As well as developing his drafting skills, he became an expert horseman and woodsman and learned the mysterious secrets of the trackless forest around him.

While George was apprenticing as a surveyor, several influential Virginians, including Augustine and Lawrence Washington, formed the Ohio Company, a land-speculation partnership whose mission was to settle families on its newly granted lands along the Ohio River. Eventually the company's holdings approached one million acres, and George found himself submerged in survey work across the wilds of Virginia.

For three years, he hiked and explored the colony, ranging as far south as the North Carolina border and as far west as the Shenandoah Valley. He camped in the open and in flea-infested backwoods cabins while he braved summer's heat and winter's cold. On one occasion, he almost drowned while attempting to cross a raging mountain stream. By the time he was eighteen, while many of his friends were attending college or pursuing mundane work, Washington had been appointed the official surveyor of Culpeper County, a position of considerable note. He had also assisted in the survey of the new town of Alexandria and saved enough money to purchase several hundred acres of prime property lying along a tributary of the Shenandoah River.

No longer a boy, he now stood over six feet tall, with reddish hair and blue-gray eyes; he weighed nearly two hundred pounds, wore a size fourteen shoe, and possessed massive hands made strong from his years of callusing labor in the wilderness. But in the midst of his youthful success, tragedy visited the young outdoorsman. His beloved half brother, Lawrence, the one person he idolized, died in 1752.

Even in death, however, Lawrence's influence continued to guide: shortly after he was laid to rest, twenty-year-old George replaced him as adjutant general of the Virginia militia with the rank of major. With no military training whatsoever, he would lead his friends and neighbors in time of war or emergency.

GEORGE WASHINGTON AND THE CHERRY TREE

Probably the most enduring myth surrounding the illustrious life of George Washington is the tale about the felling of his father's favorite cherry tree. The creator of the spurious story was Mason Locke Weems, an Anglican clergyman and part-time book agent for the noted Philadelphia publishing firm of Mathew Carey. Weems also fancied himself as a writer and in 1800 published a book entitled *The Life and Memorable Actions of George Washington*. The first biography to appear after Washington's death the previous year, it was extremely popular in the United States and abroad and throughout its life appeared in more than seventy-five printings.

The cherry-tree episode first emerged in the book's "improved" fifth edition, published with a slightly modified title in Augusta, Georgia, in 1806. Although Weems contended that he was told of the incident twenty years earlier by one of Washington's aged relatives, there is no other foundation for its truth. More likely, he invented the story to make a point to young readers that they should model their lives upon truth and honor, similar to the exemplary and unblemished life led by the first president.

In any event, the imaginative Weems portrayed young George's father as quite upset to learn that one of his most promising English cherry trees had been completely de-barked and was therefore likely to perish. When he questioned his six-year-old son, the future president declared, "I can't tell a lie, Pa; you know I can't tell a lie. I did cut it with my hatchet." The proud father responded, "Run to my arms, you dearest boy. Run to my arms; glad am I, George, that you killed my tree; for you have paid me for it a thousand fold. Such an act of heroism in my son, is more worth than a thousand trees, though blossomed with silver, and their fruits of purest gold."

"A Charming Field for
an Encounter"

A s the 1750s approached, the French population in North America stood at around fifty thousand, while the aggregate of English settlers neared the one million mark. With these rapidly growing numbers, rumors of troubling times ahead ran rampant among the Indian tribes of the upper Ohio River. Great Britain and France were on a collision course over the issue of who actually possessed the region, consisting of much of today's states of Pennsylvania, Ohio, West Virginia, and Kentucky. Of course, the hapless natives were the real possessors, although few American Indians believed in the concept of private land ownership; to them, the land was for all to share equally. As the two European giants positioned themselves for control, the Indians worried, correctly, that they would end up the eventual losers in any conflict that might ensue.

For years, control of the Ohio River valley had been irrelevant, since few settlers had encroached upon the vast wilderness with intentions of permanently occupying it. In 1747 and 1749, however, the formation of two land-speculation concerns, the Ohio Company and the Loyal Company, caught France's attention. The companies' goal was made clear to Frenchmen and Indians alike: they would introduce hundreds of settlers into the region.

French authorities reacted quickly. Even before news of the Ohio Company's charter reached them, they had dispatched an expedition from Lake Erie to survey the holdings claimed by France and to mark them appropriately. At regular intervals throughout the Ohio Valley, lead plates were buried proclaiming possession of all the land along the entire length of the Ohio River, all of the streams that entered it, and all of the land on either side of such tributaries. Now, threatened by the two Virginia land-speculation companies, French military leaders redoubled their efforts to prevent a British takeover.

During the next few years, because of heightened uneasiness between colonial administrators of the two European powers, only a small number of families moved into the new territory. The migration of hundreds of settlers, as envisioned by Ohio Company officials, failed to materialize. Even so, France took the British threat as an opportunity to send engineers throughout the region to locate sites for additional forts along the frontier. Eventually, they built several of these posts to strengthen the French position, among them, Fort Presque Isle, Fort LeBoeuf, and Fort Duquesne in Pennsylvania, and Fort Carillon (later renamed Fort Ticonderoga by the British) in New York. By the mid-1750s, tensions between the French and British governments ran high.

In the fall of 1753, Washington, then twenty-one and a major in the Virginia militia, received orders from the colony's lieutenant governor, Robert Dinwiddie, to prepare for an important journey. His travels would carry him to Fort LeBoeuf, headquarters of Legardeur de Saint-Pierre, the French military commander, where he would deliver a letter from Dinwiddie protesting the foreign presence. "It is a matter of equal concern and surprise to me, to hear that a body of French forces are erecting fortresses and making settlements . . . within his Majesty's domains," Dinwiddie declared, adding, "It becomes my duty to require your peaceable departure." Washington, both excited and apprehensive, grasped the significance of his mission and wisely secured the services of Christopher Gist, a renowned frontier scout, to guide him through the dense Virginia and Pennsylvania backwoods.

On October 31, 1753, the small militia party left Williamsburg, Virginia, and for the next month, Washington, Gist, and their companions endured severely cold weather as they made their way slowly northwestward toward the Forks of the Ohio River to the site of present-day Pittsburgh. While there, Washington made a mental note that the place would be ideal for a fort, since any structure built there would have "absolute command of both rivers." As anticipated by the young Virginian, this strategic location would soon become the site of the French Fort Duquesne and, somewhat later, the British Fort Pitt.

Upon leaving the Forks of the Ohio, Washington and his party pushed on through the frigid weather until they reached Fort LeBoeuf, near the New York border, on December 11. The

French commander responded to Lieutenant Governor Din-widdie's letter on the fourteenth, and Washington departed two days later, homeward bound for Williamsburg. At the Governor's Palace in mid-January 1754, he watched as Dinwiddie read the Frenchman's response. Saint-Pierre refused to surrender his post: "As to the summons you send me to retire, I do not think myself obliged to obey it." Saint-Pierre was much impressed with Washington, however, declaring that he had received him "with a distinction suitable to your dignity and his quality and great merit."

The die had been cast. French military authorities had no intention of voluntarily evacuating the Ohio River valley, nor were the British going to allow them to stay. There remained only one additional incident—again involving young Washington—to set the stage for war.

Less than three months after Washington returned from Fort LeBoeuf with the disappointing news that the French refused to leave the Ohio Valley, Dinwiddie prepared his friend, now promoted to lieutenant colonel, for a second mission. The lieutenant governor had been busy attempting to convince his superiors in London of the dire situation existing in the colonies. He had forwarded to England Washington's journal of the Fort LeBoeuf trip, along with the French reply, and requested additional funds for outfitting the militia. To his surprise, Parliament authorized ten thousand pounds for the containment of French ambitions in North America.

Washington's new mission again carried him north, this time to defend the frontier against a large French army rumored to be approaching from Canada. His primary responsibility was to cut a road through the Virginia, Maryland, and Pennsylvania wilderness upon which his own militia, as well as any British military forces that might arrive later, could advance toward the upper Ohio River valley. He led two militia companies, about 160 men, when he left Alexandria, Virginia, on April 2, 1754.

By the end of April, he learned that a company of Virginians, dispatched earlier to the Forks of the Ohio to build a British fort there, had been confronted by a one-thousand-man French army and forced to evacuate their recently completed post. Dismayed by the news but assured by Dinwiddie that additional troops would be forthcoming to reinforce his small contingent of soldiers, Washington pushed on, his command augmented now by several friendly Iroquois Indians. In late May, they reached a place in western Pennsylvania called Great Meadows. There, his men built a small camp consisting of wagons placed between two natural trenches, with the surrounding brush cleared for improved vision. Satisfied with the handiwork, Washington described the place as "a charming field for an encounter."

During the third day's encampment at Great Meadows, Christopher Gist reported that a French patrol had raided a nearby village. A few soldiers were dispatched to look for the Frenchmen, and after an Indian came into camp and revealed the location of the French bivouac, Washington quickly gathered forty men and marched all night in a torrential rain to meet the enemy.

At 7 A.M. on May 27, the lieutenant colonel and his tired, wet, and hungry followers peered down into a forested ravine in which the Frenchmen had pitched camp. The soldiers were eating breakfast when one of them spotted the Virginians at the top of the ravine and called out to his fellows to defend themselves. The French grabbed their arms as Washington's militiamen fired into their midst. In less than fifteen minutes, ten Frenchmen, including the patrol's commander, Joseph Coulon, sieur de Jumonville, lay dead. Twenty-one others were taken prisoner, and some of the dead and wounded were scalped by Washington's Iroquois allies before he could stop them. At least one French soldier escaped and returned to Fort Duquesne, the recently completed fort at the Forks of the Ohio, where he reported the incident to his superiors.

Washington and his men fell back to Great Meadows. Along the way, he received news that he had been promoted to colonel and commander of all Virginia forces. At the Meadows, he supervised the strengthening of the camp, surrounding it with a palisade of strong timbers. Although no detailed portrayal of the fort has survived, Washington himself described it as "a small temporary stockade in the middle of the entrenchment called Fort Necessity, erected for the sole purpose of [the] security [of the powder] and of the few stores we had."

He waited tensely at Fort Necessity for the confrontation; then, during the early-morning hours of July 3, in a raging rainstorm, three columns of French troops attacked. After a day of fierce fighting, Washington realized that his small force was no match for the numerically superior French. Just past midnight on

July 4, 1754, he surrendered. His casualties included thirty killed and seventy wounded. He had lost the first battle of what would become known as the French and Indian War, inspiring the English man of letters Horace Walpole to declare, "The volley fired by a young Virginian in the backwoods of America set the world on fire."

"I Heard the Bullets Whistle. . . . There Is Something Charming in the Sound"

For a man unaccustomed to military affairs, George Washington had adapted well to his first experience as a soldier in combat. Following the skirmish with the French patrol in which Jumonville was killed, he wrote excitedly from his camp at Great Meadows to a younger brother, "I heard the bullets whistle, and, believe me, there is something charming in the sound." He was pleased when his friends and neighbors gave him a hero's welcome, honoring him with near-celebrity status upon his return to Virginia from Fort Necessity. Yet he was still troubled that he had lost the battle, and a ticklish issue regarding the surrender terms he had signed with the French clouded his otherwise gala reception.

The problem arose from the faulty translation of a word in the surrender document. When the papers were presented to British officials in London, they were horrified to discover that the young colonel had mistakenly admitted "assassinating" Jumonville, rather than acknowledging that the Frenchman had simply been "killed" in combat. The issue, which nearly became an international incident, was resolved in the end, and Washington's future in the military remained secure.

He realized that if he wanted to achieve success in the army, he had to recognize the political implications that were attached to it. Soon after his return from Fort Necessity, the British high command reorganized the Virginia militia, proclaiming that the highest rank attainable was captain. A decree was also issued classifying colonial militia officers inferior to British army regulars of the same rank. If Washington were to stay in the militia, he faced a demotion and the loss of three grades, along with the associated pay and prestige. He angrily declared that he would also be outranked by "every Captain, bearing the King's commission, every half-pay officer, or other, appearing with such a commission."

By November 1754, he had learned all he wanted to know of reorganization, loss of rank, and similar army matters. Although he had served Virginia well and revealed in his resignation letter that his inclinations were "strongly bent to arms," he nevertheless took his leave of the Virginia militia and rode off to Mount Vernon, which he leased on December 10 from the widow of his late half brother, Lawrence. There, at the place he loved more than any other spot on earth, he would weigh his future and formulate plans for the transformation of the plantation into a showplace on the Potomac.

In late February 1755, a crowd of curious spectators gathered on the wharf at Hampton Roads, Virginia, to watch as several

British warships tied up at the docks. The ships had left Cork, Ireland, the previous December and carried two regiments of British infantry—the Forty-fourth and Forty-eighth—both undermanned, but still numbering around one thousand soldiers. The red-coated troops reported to Major General Edward Braddock, a sixty-year-old veteran of the elite Coldstream Guards; with forty years of military service, he was the newly appointed commander in chief of all British forces in North America. Following Colonel Washington's embarrassing surrender at Great Meadows the previous July, King George II had instructed the general to teach the upstart French a thing or two. Braddock was apprehensive about the assignment; before his departure to Virginia, he confided to a friend in London that she would never see him again.

After moving his army to Alexandria, Virginia, Braddock and his staff proceeded to Williamsburg, where he met with Lieutenant Governor Dinwiddie to map out the strategy he would follow in expelling the French from America. His personal orders included marching an army through the backwoods of Virginia, Maryland, and Pennsylvania and forcing the French to evacuate Fort Duquesne.

At Mount Vernon, meantime, Washington wondered if Braddock's presence upon the scene of what now appeared to be a rapidly developing, all-out war with France, would make any real difference. The general certainly had an illustrious reputation, and he just might provide the type of leadership the young Virginian could follow. In the ensuing days, Washington launched a discreet investigation to determine if Braddock had any interest in recruiting him for service. On March 14, his curiosity ended when he received a letter from Braddock's aide-de-camp inviting him to join the general's staff. He was advised that he need not be concerned with the issue of colonial vs. regular officers and their relationship to each other, since "all inconveniences of that kind [the problem of rank] will be obviated." On April 1, Washington accepted a volunteer position on Braddock's staff, without rank or pay.

In April at Alexandria, following weeks of intensive logistical planning, frantic recruiting, and assembly of horses, wagons, and other war matériel, Braddock reviewed his command. The addition of conscripts from Virginia and other colonies had augmented the force to around 2,500 men. Thirty members of the Royal Navy, six hundred poorly nourished horses, a variety of artillery pieces, and a large number of wagoners, axmen, mechanics, and blacksmiths rounded out his army.

On April 14, the British leader held one last meeting with Dinwiddie and the governors of several other colonies, at which time he revealed the final strategy for the prosecution of the war against the French and their ouster from North America. Conceived months earlier in England by the Crown's military ministers, it was to be a grand, three-pronged effort. Braddock was first to secure Fort Duquesne at the Forks of the Ohio River. Then a colonial army would invade New York, focusing on the Great Lakes region and attempting to capture Fort Niagara and the string of French posts along the Niagara River. Finally, the French stronghold, Fort St. Frédéric, strategically situated at the southern end of Lake Champlain, had to be captured or destroyed.

Later in the spring, Braddock marched his army out of Alexandria, bound for the staging area at Fort Cumberland, Maryland, more than one hundred miles northwest. The force arrived on May 10, the same day Washington was named Braddock's aide-de-camp. By early June the British commander decided that his soldiers were ready, and he dispatched three hundred axmen to begin clearing the road. The easy part of the journey, getting this far from Alexandria through largely settled territory, was over; now the real difficulties began—hacking through more than one hundred miles of practically impenetrable forest between Fort Cumberland and the Forks of the Ohio.

By June 10, all of Braddock's command had departed Fort Cumberland, but though the trees along the way had been felled, the army still had to cope with stumps, thick underbrush, and steep mountain defiles, all of which conspired to slow to a snail's pace the movement of the wagons and artillery caissons. Braddock complained that the primitive countryside was nothing short of "an uninhabited wilderness of steep rocky mountains and almost impassable morasses."

Alarmed by the army's amazingly slow progress, Washington suggested to his commander that the majority of wagons and some of the artillery be left behind, temporarily, thereby allowing a contingent of infantrymen to advance more rapidly toward Fort Duquesne. Then, he reasoned, the wagons with the heavy supplies could bring up the rear. Braddock agreed and on June 19 he and Washington, with about 1,200 soldiers, a few wagons, and a large number of packhorses, split from the rest of the command. In a letter to his brother, Washington confided disgustedly that his joy at the prospect of picking up speed was soon dampened when the soldiers halted "to level every mole-hill, and to build bridges over every brook, by which means we were four days in getting twelve miles."

For almost three more weeks, the tired, hungry, and disenchanted troops labored through the thick Pennsylvania woods. Washington, in the meantime, had contracted dysentery and fallen behind the main column. By July 7, Braddock's troops reached the Monongahela River, one of the Ohio's major tributaries, at a point just upstream from the mouth of Turtle Creek and about ten miles from their destination. The route that the general followed required his men to cross the river twice, but both times they did so without incident. Two days later, they were within seven miles of the enemy fortress. Although still ill, Washington finally arrived at Braddock's command post after being transported in a wagon for miles along the primitive road.

Grateful but surprised that the French had not ambushed the column as it crossed the river, Braddock ordered his men to take a brief rest and reminded his staff to be on the watch for an attack. The words were barely spoken when nearly nine hundred French regulars, Canadians, and French-allied Indians—among them Hurons, Ottawas, Shawnees, Iroquois, and Ojibways—exploded from the surrounding forest. Rifles boomed and arrows and tomahawks flew through the air as scores of dead and wounded British and colonial soldiers fell.

The conflict, known as the Battle of the Wilderness, lasted for more than three hours. General Braddock lost four horses, shot out from under him, and Washington later gratefully wrote to his brother, "I had 4 Bullets through my Coat, and two Horses shot under me, and yet escaped unhurt." Braddock realized he had lost the fight and barked out orders to retreat. As he did, he fell in the thick undergrowth, mortally wounded. With their leader disabled, many terrified British soldiers deserted the field, continuing the retreat for the next several days toward the rear guard, which was still slowly making its way to the battle scene.

Braddock died four days later, on July 13, and was buried in the middle of the road that his men had cut through the wilderness. The heavy activity of retreating men and animals obliterated all evidence of the grave so that the enemy could not desecrate it. In addition to the commander in chief and sixty-two other officers, nearly nine hundred British and colonial soldiers died or were wounded in this, the first major battle of the still undeclared French and Indian War. Washington estimated that no more than thirty Virginians remained alive out of three companies. The French and Indians suffered only fifty-six casualties.

Following the battle, Washington criticized the British army's conduct, writing to his mother that their behavior "exposed all those who were inclined to do their duty to almost certain death." However, he said, his fellow Virginians "behaved like men, and died like soldiers."

"I Would Be a Willing Offering to Savage Fury"

One of Washington's recent biographers, James Thomas Flexner, described the bloody defeat of General Braddock's British and Virginia troops at the hands of the French and Indians near the Forks of the Ohio River in July 1755, as "the most catastrophic in all Anglo-American history." The massacre certainly left British authorities in London searching for new ways to expel their French foes from North America. In the meantime, Washington and his detractors blamed one another for the debacle. He maintained that the battle could have been won had Braddock not denied him partial command of the British column, allowing him to blend into the wilderness "and engage the enemy in their own way." The Crown's generals, on the other hand, held Washington responsible for corrupting their soldiers' discipline when he criticized their use of age-old European battle formations instead of adopting wilderness-style guerrilla tactics.

The momentous French victory left possession of the strategic Fort Duquesne and the surrounding region in enemy hands, and British authorities soon shifted their focus from western Pennsylvania to the northern colonies, leaving the remote Virginia frontier defenseless. The remnant of Braddock's army limped off to Philadelphia, while a still seriously ill Washington rode to Mount Vernon to consider his future. He was encouraged when his Virginia neighbors gave him another hero's welcome, enjoying the praise and notoriety heaped upon him, but he was still troubled by the hard choices he had to make. Would he leave the army and devote himself to his agricultural chores at Mount Vernon, or should he remain with the British and help expel the hated French from North America?

If he was having difficulty deciding which pathway to take, members of the Virginia General Assembly had no qualms about assisting him with his choice. They quickly organized a colonial army and named the master of Mount Vernon "Colonel of the Virginia Regiment and Commander in Chief of all Virginia forces." The lawmakers were happy to give Washington complete authority over the new regiment and authorized him to raise between 1,200 and 2,000 soldiers, select his own officer corps, provide for equipment and supplies, and immediately set into motion the defense of the frontier.

To further complicate Washington's career decisions, the old question of who outranked whom in the military chain of command reemerged. Maryland's royal governor, Horatio Sharpe, maintained that one of his own men, Captain John Dagworthy, a one-time British army regular, outranked Washington. Sharpe declared that the young colonel would henceforth take his orders from Dagworthy. Virginia's chief executive, Robert Dinwiddie, appealed to William Shirley, the governor of Massachusetts and the Crown's acting North American commander in chief, to recognize Washington as the superior officer. At the same time, he suggested to Shirley that the entire issue might be resolved once and for all if the Virginia militia unit were merged into the regular British army. Even though Washington traveled to Massachusetts to argue his case personally, the issue was never settled to his satisfaction. Shirley not only ignored Dinwiddie's pleas but went a step further: henceforth, the Virginia regiment would report to a new unit, to be commanded by Maryland's Governor Sharpe.

Once again, Washington considered resigning his commission and retiring to the privacy of Mount Vernon. When he returned from Boston, however, he was faced with yet another crisis on the frontier and hastened to Winchester to confront an Indian attack. Weeks passed into months while the bloodshed continued. Despite his best diplomatic, organizational, and recruiting skills, he could not prevent the Shenandoah Valley from becoming immersed in all-out war with the French-allied Indian tribes in the region. He found his new militia recruits to be petty and trifling, totally inept at the rigorous training that his officers demanded. Food supplies, always an issue, dwindled significantly as the army's population swelled in numbers yet decreased in quality. Saddened by his inability to defend the pioneer families who looked to him for protection, Washington dejectedly wrote, "If bleeding, dying! Would glut their insatiate revenge, I would be a willing offering to savage fury, and die by inches to save a people!"

In July 1757, during some of King George II's most embarrassing moments over continued British military reverses in North America and India, William Pitt the Elder became prime minister. A strong, well-qualified, no-nonsense statesman, Pitt grasped iron control of the government, determined to win the protracted American war with France. His strategy was similar to that of the ill-fated General Braddock. Montreal and Quebec would be captured, the French-held forts in New York would be taken, and the large, well-entrenched garrison at Fort Duquesne would be defeated and expelled. The part of this plan that interested Washington was the occupation of Fort Duquesne.

By January 1758, rumors circulated in Williamsburg that the commander of the Fort Duquesne campaign would be John Forbes, a former medical student, career soldier, and adjutant to John Campbell, fourth earl of Loudoun, who, as commander in chief of all British North American forces, had demonstrated little understanding of the Crown's American problems. Forbes received his commission in March and within two months had recruited nearly six thousand troops, including colonials from North Carolina, Virginia, Pennsylvania, and Maryland, plus a contingent of around six hundred Cherokee and Catawba tribesmen.

As much as Washington liked what he heard about Forbes, it

bothered him to learn that the new commander was considering opening a new road from the Pennsylvania frontier settlements due west to Fort Duquesne. After all, had not Washington's militia—in 1754 during the Fort Necessity campaign, and again the following year with General Edward Braddock—extended the road from Alexandria to Fort Cumberland and nearly to the Forks? Would it not be far simpler for Forbes to launch his new offensive from Alexandria as well, retracing the route of these earlier forays? Why would Forbes even consider a change in the debarkation site, one that required him to blaze a second wide swath through more than one hundred miles of fresh wilderness and across five mountain ranges and nearly a score of rivers and streams?

Despite Washington's reasoning on the proper route to the Forks, Forbes won the argument and decreed that a new road would indeed be opened across southern Pennsylvania. By early July, he had assembled his army at Raystown, where it joined forces with some of the Virginia militia, as well as a few troops from the Carolinas and Maryland who had marched overland from Fort Cumberland. In the meantime, Forbes, seriously ill with the "flux" (dysentery), was forced to stay behind at Carlisle, while his second-in-command, Colonel Henry Bouquet, took control of the army.

In mid-September 1758, following an abortive British raid on Fort Duquesne during which nearly one-half of Bouquet's attackers were killed, the French commander of the post, Captain François-Marie de Marchand, Sieur de Ligneris, heightened security and braced the garrison for what he assumed would be an all-out attack. He soon learned, however, that a few weeks earlier the important French command post, Fort Frontenac, poised on Lake Ontario to protect shipping on the St. Lawrence River, had been destroyed by the British. The captain realized the significance of the loss: Fort Duquesne was now totally isolated from the French supply lines upon which he depended for food, ammunition, and other war matériel. With no sources of resupply, did it make sense to maintain his tiny garrison of only five hundred troops and attempt to defend the fort against the approaching six-thousand-man British army?

De Ligneris then made a strange, fateful decision: he would attack the British on their own ground. In mid-October, he dispatched a force, consisting of practically the entire garrison at Fort Duquesne, to nearby Fort Ligonier, a small post that had been hastily built by the British on the road to the Forks. Although severely outnumbered, the French troops fought valiantly, and their conduct greatly contributed to Forbes's decision, on November 11, to delay the attack on Fort Duquesne until the following spring. In another French attack the next day, Washington's Virginia regiment, together with another British unit, engaged the enemy in darkness, resulting in a sizable casualty rate from friendly fire. During the brief encounter, a prisoner was taken who admitted to his captors that Fort Duquesne was badly undermanned and certainly nowhere near the strength assumed by Forbes and his lieutenants.

The prisoner's revelation changed the plans of the British commanders, who now agreed that the time was right for an all-out attack upon the French fortification. By November 22, with Washington at the head of his Virginians and Colonel Bouquet bringing up the artillery, the British force camped within twelve miles of the Forks.

Captain de Ligneris, in the meantime, had no intention of leaving any supplies, equipment, or other matériel for the British to capture. He gave orders to dismantle the fort, destroy the stockade posts, tear down the internal housing, and ship the artillery down the Ohio to Fort Massac. Fifty barrels of black powder were arranged inside the former stockade and ignited. With a few days' rations, his brave troopers marched off to Fort Machault, a few miles to the north.

When the British saw the dark clouds of smoke on the western horizon, they hurried to the Forks only to find a smoldering heap of ashes where Fort Duquesne formerly stood. General Forbes, still suffering from dysentery, traveled to the front to take personal command of his army and, together with Washington and several other senior officers, entered the parade ground and proudly watched as the Union Jack was hoisted to the top of a nearby flagpole. Washington could barely wait to notify Virginia's governor, Francis Fauquier, of the news. "I have the pleasure to inform you that Fort Duquesne, or the ground rather on which it stood, was possessed by his Majesty's troops on the 25th instant. The enemy . . . burned the fort, and ran away at night."

On the following day, Forbes ordered that the fortification, to be rebuilt by his engineers, would henceforth be called Fort Pitt, in honor of his patron, the British prime minister. The general's illness required that he be carried on a litter all the way to Philadelphia, where he died less than six months later.

As for Washington, he declared that he was retiring from the army and going home to his beloved Mount Vernon.

"Enquire . . . in the Neighborhood, & Get Some Egg's and Chickens"

In March 1758, eight months before the fall of Fort Duquesne and his subsequent retirement from the Virginia militia, George Washington met Martha Dandridge Custis, a wealthy widow, nearly a year his senior and mistress of the White House Plantation, a large estate near Williamsburg. Her marriage in 1749 to Colonel Daniel Parke Custis, and his death following a brief illness seven years later, had left her with two small children, John and Martha. Mrs. Custis was a native Virginian, born in New Kent County, just a few miles from Washington's own birthplace. Standing barely more than five feet tall, she was dwarfed by her suitor's immense frame.

That George and Martha were ideally paired seems beyond question—their devotion to one another and the duration of their marriage attests to it. Historians have, however, speculated on what drew the retired militiaman to the popular widow, specifically what influence her great wealth had upon their quick courtship. Her estate consisted of nearly eighteen thousand acres of prime Virginia farmland spread across six counties and divided into several plantations. These holdings, together with her slaves, homes, farm buildings, livestock, and town properties in Williamsburg, represented affluence as well as influence on Virginia society.

Although Washington himself controlled thousands of acres of Virginia land, either through lease arrangements or outright ownership, his prolonged absences from home during the French and Indian War and the debts that had accumulated in the day-to-day operations of his plantation had left him cash-poor. With his marriage to Martha, he took control of her sizable holdings, explaining in a letter to his London agent, "I am entitled to a third part of that [the Custis] Estate, and invested likewise with the care of the other two thirds by a Decree of our Genl. Court which I obtain'd in order to strengthen the Power I before had in consequences of my Wifes Administration." Realistically, the marriage made Washington an instant millionaire, and he realized that he could put the new funds to good use in the restoration project at Mount Vernon that he had begun two years earlier.

Washington's romance with Martha was not his first. While still a teenager, he had written passionate poetry to an unnamed neighborhood beauty and later, smitten again, confided to a friend his joy in the company of "a very agreeable Young Lady." He also seriously courted Elizabeth "Betsy" Fauntleroy, a young Virginia woman of high social standing in the colony. In a letter dated

May 20, 1752, he wrote Betsy's father, imploring his assistance in gaining his daughter's acceptance. Sadly, the epistle was never answered and a lovesick Washington finally gave up on the lady.

Other than Martha, the one serious love of his life was Sally Fairfax, the wife of his friend George Fairfax and a sister-in-law of his half brother, Lawrence. From the time the eighteen-year-old beauty arrived at Belvoir to marry Fairfax, Washington, two years her junior, had been infatuated by her beauty and charm. Through the years, the pair appeared to enjoy a platonic relationship. Once, while on sick leave at Mount Vernon during the late war with the French and Indians, Washington called on Sally to comfort him, a request she gladly fulfilled. And, remarkably, during the brief period between his engagement and marriage to Martha, he wrote a letter to Sally in which he proclaimed, "The World has no business to know the object of my Love, declard in this manner to you when I want to conceal it." Although nothing illicit about their relationship has ever been discovered, and Sally later moved abroad in apparent happiness with her husband, she and Washington remained friends until his death.

Washington and Martha Custis married on January 6, 1759, just a few weeks after his return to Virginia from victory at the Forks of the Ohio. Thus began a forty-year marriage that, according to historian George E. Ross, was "one of mutual love, respect, and admiration that grew stronger with the years." The vows were exchanged at St. Peter's Church in New Kent County with the Reverend John Mossum officiating. The bride wore a white silk dress, decorated with diamonds and pearls, and the groom was attired in a blue suit with silver ornaments. Following the wedding, Martha was escorted back to White House Plantation in a carriage drawn by six horses, Washington and his attendants riding horseback alongside her.

Following closely on the wedding, Washington took his seat in the House of Burgesses, the lower chamber of the General Assembly. As early as 1755, he had explored the possibility of representing his home county of Fairfax but was dissuaded from actually entering the contest when it appeared that men of higher social status were favored for the two available seats. He had also investigated, to no avail, running for the same office from Frederick County, where he owned property and, in 1758, while he was absent participating in the campaign to capture Fort Duquesne, he again allowed his name to be placed on the ballot there. He won the election handily, by a vote of 309 to 88 for the closest opponent. Since he now had to report to Williamsburg to attend the House of Burgesses's first session of the year, he and Martha decided to spend their honeymoon in the capital city, at one of the Custis properties.

The House of Burgesses dated to Virginia's earliest beginnings. The legislative body met twice each year and, like a state's legislature today, its members considered any and all items of interest and import to the colony. An early example of democracy in action, the House of Burgesses had members who were elected by popular vote but invariably hailed from the landed gentry of the colony. Historian Carl Bridenbaugh called the institution "a tobacco planter's club," adding, "For over half a century 'gentlemen of the best families and fortunes' had been consciously coalescing into an exclusive ruling class." It was well known that those who campaigned for the chamber were not beyond influencing their constituents' decisions with gifts of liquor. Even in Washington's bid in Frederick County for his first elected office, his associates, representing him at the polls in his absence, distributed more than 160 gallons of spirits, nearly one-half gallon for every voter.

Washington reported to his seat in Williamsburg on February 22, 1759, his twenty-seventh birthday. An associate described him as standing about six feet, two inches tall, and weighing 175 pounds, "straight as Indian" and possessing "well-developed muscles, indicating great strength." Furthermore, the colleague said, "His demeanor at all times [is] composed and dignified. His movements and gestures are graceful, his walk majestic, and he is a splendid horseman." He was also reportedly reserved and somewhat shy. At the House's first session, when fellow burgesses officially recognized him for his outstanding service to the King and the colony during the recent conflict with France, the embarrassed young Virginian was speechless. The speaker of the House added his gratitude and respect, reassuring Washington, "Your modesty is equal to your valor, and that surpasses the power of any language that I possess."

When the House of Burgesses completed its deliberations in late March 1759, Washington began preparations for the 150-mile journey to Mount Vernon. His entourage included Martha, the two Custis children, a variety of slaves, and sundry household items purchased in Williamsburg. When the party neared its destination, he realized that he had failed to advise the farm employees about his new family's imminent arrival. He dashed off a quick directive to his overseer, instructing him to supervise the cleaning and airing out of the rooms, the making of fires in the fireplaces, and the polishing and installation of tables, chairs, and bedsteads. "Enquire abt. in the Neighborhood, & get some Egg's and Chickens, and prepare in the best manner you can for our coming," he wrote.

Mount Vernon had changed considerably since Washington's father, Augustine, purchased the Hunting Creek Plantation from his sister in 1726 for a paltry £180. He named the farm Epsewasson, after a local creek, and soon afterward built a small, four-room house there. After Lawrence, Augustine's son, inherited the property in 1743, he renamed the estate Mount Vernon in honor of the British naval officer, Admiral Edward Vernon, under whose command he served during the late war with Spain. Within weeks, in anticipation of his marriage to Anne Fairfax, Lawrence razed his father's earlier house and replaced it with an eight-room, one-and-one-half-story frame dwelling covered with clapboard.

In 1754 George leased the estate and eighteen slaves from Lawrence's widow, Anne, for fifteen thousand pounds of tobacco, half his annual income. Three years later, he began an ambitious restoration program that would remodel and enlarge the main house and restructure the plantation to his own specifications. Now, as the carriage bearing him and his new family proceeded up the long driveway to the house, he could see the considerable progress made in his absence.

The house was nearly complete. Washington had instructed his workmen to preserve the central core of Lawrence's building, but to raise the roof to two and one-half stories. The new second floor contained five rooms, all of them with eight-foot ceilings. Small wings were also added at either end of the structure, and a new staircase dominated the impressive entrance hall. The renovation had doubled the size of the home, providing the needed space for Martha's two young children. But the most enduring of Washington's modifications was his decision to have the primary living areas face west, whereas Lawrence had preferred his home to overlook the beautiful Potomac River.

Home at last. Other than occasional trips to Williamsburg and a few personal journeys to check on his land holdings, Washington would not leave Mount Vernon for the next decade and a half. His marriage to Martha Custis had made him a wealthy man, and he now had the resources to convert his beloved home from an acceptable middle-class farm to a premier plantation comparable to those of his prosperous neighbors.

He became absorbed in agricultural matters, always with an eye toward improving the soil, increasing crop yields, and acquiring land. Tobacco was the primary cash crop in Virginia, but for the past few years its price had tumbled in London, where it had to be sold since no market existed at home. Years of continuous tobacco growing had exhausted the soil, so he began experimenting with wheat, flax, hemp, and corn as alternatives. Not only were they kinder to the earth, but they also could be marketed in America. As his ambitious plans for the future grew, so did the size of Mount Vernon and its operations. When he and Martha married, she brought with her many personal slaves and these, added to the ones already working on the farm, made the couple sizable slaveholders. The slaves, blacksmiths, carpenters, weavers, and other workers and servants who helped run large farms transformed Mount Vernon into a small community. Supervising it, Washington once remarked, was not unlike commanding an army.

Most of Virginia's affluent tidewater planters employed London agents to broker their tobacco and other agricultural products for the overseas market. These same agents also acted as buyers for the planters, normally extending a large line of credit to be paid down by proceeds from the sale of the farmer's produce. The system was basically one of honor, with no guarantees to the Virginians that their agents conducted business in the most profitable manner. In time, particularly after several failed growing seasons, it became a common occurrence for planters to become heavily indebted to their agents. Within a very few years of his marriage, Washington fell into this trap. Blinded by the assets he had derived from Martha, he greatly overextended his credit with his agent, and his solution to the financial crisis—purchasing more slaves to work more land to grow more crops—failed. By the mid-1760s, he faced bankruptcy.

"Some Thing Shou'd Be Done to . . . Maintain . . . Liberty"

Between his marriage in 1759 and 1774, Washington became an affluent and respected member of Virginia society, and his continuous reelection to the House of Burgesses made him a man of importance in both colonial and community governmental affairs. His decision to reduce Mount Vernon's production of tobacco and develop and grow alternative cash crops for local consumption eventually paid dividends and, because he could now direct the disposition of his produce, he no longer had to rely on money-hungry London agents over whom he had no control. His finances gradually improved, and the new success fired his ambitions to control even more property than the nearly ten thousand acres he already possessed.

As early as 1763, Washington traveled to the Great Dismal Swamp, located on the border separating Virginia and North Carolina. He had become interested in developing the region for farming by exposing the rich soil that had for centuries supported a luxuriant growth of marsh vegetation. His favorable impression prompted him and a few associates to organize a company and send slaves to drain parts of the vast swamp and prepare the land for crops.

Four years later, he was still interested in acquiring new properties. In 1763 King George III had issued a proclamation that no white settlement west of the crest of the Appalachian Mountains would be tolerated. Defying the Crown's decree, Washington, in 1767, wrote to a friend in western Pennsylvania urging him to try "to secure some of the most valuable Lands in the Kings part which I think may be accomplished after a while notwithstanding the Proclamation that restrains it at present & prohibits the Settling of them at all." He added cautiously, "I would recommend it to you to keep this whole matter a profound Secret, or Trust it only with those in whom you can confide & who can assist you in bringing it to bear."

In the fall of 1770, his passion to add acreage to his domain again surfaced. This time his eye turned to the free bounty lands on the western frontier, which Lieutenant Governor Robert Dinwiddie had promised to veterans of the French and Indian War in exchange for their military service. Washington and his friend Dr. James Craik explored the Ohio River valley from Fort Pitt (Pittsburgh) to the mouth of the Great Kanawha River, 160 miles downstream, where they selected and marked several parcels of prime land. Eventually, Washington amassed close to nineteen thousand acres as grants, plus another five thousand acres that he purchased from fellow veterans. With these acquisitions, his wealth, at least as far as land ownership was concerned, was restored.

To Americans, one of the most damaging consequences of the French and Indian War was the financial burden it caused Great Britain and the resultant hardships that the Crown, in turn, placed upon its colonies to help pay for the conflict. Maintaining an army halfway around the world had plunged England's treasury into a debt totaling several million pounds sterling. Keeping a presence in North America, and paying for the subsistence of ten thousand troops to monitor the peace, had cost thousands of pounds annually, money that Britain simply could not spare.

Only one solution appeared feasible to ameliorate the island nation's fiscal predicament: to levy assorted taxes on the colonies. Accordingly, on March 22, 1765, just two years after the Treaty of Paris officially ended the war, England imposed the first of such taxes in the form of the Stamp Act, the revenue generated to be used "toward defraying the expenses of defending, protecting, and securing the British colonies and plantations in America." The legislation required that a revenue stamp be purchased and placed on every article of paper used in the colonies—commercial and legal papers, insurance policies, ships' papers, pamphlets, magazines, newspapers, and other publications.

Two days later, Parliament passed another revenue-generating measure (or perhaps more accurately, a cost-cutter), the Quartering Act, whereby the Crown hoped to defray some of the expenses of maintaining its troops in America. Suddenly, colonists discovered that they were required by royal edict to furnish food, shelter, and supplies to British soldiers quartered in their neighborhoods. And in June 1767, yet another tax was added to the colonists' burden with the passage of the Townshend Revenue Act, which placed duties on such imported items as paper, glass, paint, and tea.

The angry colonial response to these laws was no surprise to the British government. In addition to physical attacks on the Crown's tax collectors, citizens simply refused to comply with the taxations. American leaders denounced them all, with one of the most vocal voices being that of John Adams, a Massachusetts lawyer who called the Stamp Act "that enormous engine fabricated by the British Parliament, for battering down all the rights and liberties of America." When Patrick Henry, a young, self-educated attorney and recently elected delegate, protested the Stamp Act in Virginia's House of Burgesses in May 1765, the speaker declared his speech "Treason!" The truculent Henry replied, "If this be treason, make the most of it."

Washington served as a burgess at the time, but his correspondence reveals little insight into his thoughts on the taxes and their impact upon the colonies. At first his interests were localized, but as time passed, he became increasingly anti-British. Soon after the implementation of the Stamp Act, he timidly admitted that his friends and neighbors "look upon this unconstitutional method of Taxation as a direful attack upon their Liberties, and loudly exclaim against the Violation." Four years later, however, his stance had toughened: "At a time when our lordly Masters in Great Britain will be satisfied with nothing less than the deprivation of American freedom, it seems highly necessary that some thing shou'd be done to avert the stroke and maintain the liberty which we have derived from our Ancestors; but the manner of doing it to answer the purpose effectually is the point in question." Just as, a few years earlier, he had broken his personal economic ties to England, he now foresaw the dawning of a time when more serious colonial relationships would be terminated as well.

In May 1769, the Virginia House of Burgesses sitting in Williamsburg passed a resolution declaring that only the colonial government had the authority to tax its citizens. Upon receiving the act for signature, the governor, Norborne Berkeley, baron de Botetourt, adjourned the House. Members immediately reconvened down the street at Raleigh Tavern, where, with an angered Washington in the forefront, they passed another resolution urging Virginians to boycott taxed items from Great Britain.

Tensions ran high between colonists and British soldiers in Boston as the spring of 1770 approached. On March 5, when a contrived confrontation between a group of American trouble seekers and a small contingent of the Crown's troops occurred, the possibilities of turning the disturbance into an international incident could not be overlooked by the beleaguered colonists. Sam Adams, a Boston activist and cousin of John Adams, masterminded the incident in which rock-throwing Americans attacked the supposedly peaceable British soldiers. In the confusion, the redcoats opened fire, killing five colonists and severely wounding six others. Adams capitalized on the fracas, called the Boston Massacre, and turned it into a major news event. As affairs turned out, a colonial jury eventually acquitted the soldiers when its members perceived that the redcoats had been lured into the conflict.

Following the Boston Massacre, relations between Great Britain and the American colonies continued to deteriorate, climaxing on the night of December 16, 1773, when several Bostonians dressed as Indians gathered at Griffin's Wharf. There, they boarded three

British ships and threw 342 chests of tea, valued at eighteen thousand pounds sterling into the harbor. British officials immediately closed all shipping in and out of Boston and eventually passed a series of what colonists called "Intolerable Acts," aimed at punishing the perpetrators. Washington personally disapproved of the Boston Tea Party, but he also disdained the "despotick measures" taken by the British in retaliation.

In May 1774, the House of Burgesses once again passed resolutions denouncing the Crown's unfair taxation of American colonists and, once again, the governor, now John Murray, the earl of Dunmore, disbanded the body. As in earlier times, the burgesses met at Raleigh Tavern and set the stage for convening the First Continental Congress to deal with the problems common to all the colonies.

The Congress would assemble in Philadelphia in September. During the summer before his departure for the meeting, Washington found the time to add a large wing to his Mount Vernon home, rendering the residence temporarily unsymmetrical until he could build a similar addition on the other side two years later. He also assisted in the disposal of the household furnishings at Belvoir, home of his lifelong friend, George Fairfax, and his wife, Sally, who had recently moved to England, and he found the time to write a revealing letter to a loyalist friend outlining his growing hostility toward the Crown. "I think the Parliament of Great Britain hath no more right to put their hands into my pocket, without my consent," he declared, "than I have to put my hands into yours for money; and this being already urged to them in a firm, but decent manner, by all the colonies, what reason is there to expect any thing from their justice?"

Washington left Mount Vernon in late August and arrived in Philadelphia in mid-September. A vibrant town of nearly twenty-four thousand, Philadelphia was America's largest city, with a college, six newspapers, a score of churches of nearly all denominations, forty silversmiths, fourteen rum distilleries, and seven sugar refineries.

Washington's friend Peyton Randolph, speaker of the Virginia House of Burgesses, was elected president of the Congress. The rest of the Virginia delegation consisted of Richard Bland, Patrick Henry, Richard Henry Lee, Edmund Pendleton, Benjamin Harrison, and Washington. The meetings convened in Carpenters' Hall, owned by the Carpenters' Company, a fifty-year-old brotherhood of tradesmen. When the town's loyalists heard of the impending use of the structure by the newly formed Continental Congress, they threatened the Carpenters' membership, vowing that the hall might be confiscated and that "their necks might be inconveniently lengthened." Undaunted, the brotherhood allowed the meetings on their property anyway.

During Congress's first session, many discussions were held and a myriad of plans were studied, but little progress was made. The representatives returned to their homes on October 26 with no clear-cut idea of how to resolve the deteriorating affairs with Great Britain. Before they recessed, however, they agreed to meet again the following May to continue their efforts. As spring arrived, new developments in Massachusetts made it clear that war between the American colonies and Great Britain would not be long coming.

In April 1775, General Thomas Gage, the Crown's military

commander in North America, learned that militiamen near Boston had armed themselves and were stockpiling weapons and supplies. On the eighteenth, he dispatched seven hundred troops to Concord to confiscate the war matériel, and on the following day, eight American minutemen were shot and killed by British redcoats at nearby Lexington. News of the conflict in Massachusetts reached Washington at Mount Vernon on April 27. He hesitatingly departed his plantation on May 4, again bound for Philadelphia and the Second Continental Congress, where a future and a fate, both unimaginable to him as his driver pointed the carriage northward, awaited.

During the past two years, while great political and social unrest was stirring in America, Washington's family suffered a personal tragedy. Soon after his marriage to Martha, he had adopted John Parke (called "Jackie"), aged four, and Martha Parke (called "Patsy"), aged two, and treated them as his own. He once declared that he believed a heavier burden lay with a guardian such as himself than with a natural parent. He doted on the children, and deliveries from his London brokers unloaded at Alexandria or Mount Vernon always included something—clothing, dolls, toys, or sweets—for the pair.

When Patsy was twelve, she sustained a serious injury from a fall. An examination revealed that she suffered from epilepsy, a condition that caused her indulgent parents to further spoil her. Five years later, in June 1773, while "in better health and spirits than she appeared to have been in for some time," wrote Washington to Martha's brother-in-law, she rose from the dinner table and within two minutes dropped dead. "This sudden, and unexpected blow, I scarce need add has reduced my poor Wife to the lowest ebb of Misery," he lamented.

Jackie, in the meantime, proved a disappointment to his mother and stepfather. Always lazy and unmotivated, he showed little interest in serious matters, instead spending his time and money on horses and clothes. In mid-1773 Washington had him admitted to King's College (present-day Columbia University) in New York City, but, bored with his studies, he soon left school and married socially prominent Eleanor Calvert of Maryland. With the death of her daughter and the absence of her son, Martha sank into deep depression. It worsened when she lost the presence, love, and support of her husband as he departed Mount Vernon for Philadelphia and what lay beyond.

"I Do Not Think My-Self Equal to the Command I Am Honored With"

The Second Continental Congress convened on May 10, 1775, and for days the delegates argued, trying to define reasonable but effective measures to invoke against Great Britain. The skirmishes in Concord and Lexington the previous month had hardened the Massachusetts delegation's resolve and, led by John Adams, an attorney who had defended the British soldiers arrested during the Boston Massacre, its members urged the other colonies to lend them military assistance for the expected reprisals.

Despite the martial overtones of the meeting, those attending realized that if war really came to America, the colonies would be hard-pressed to defend themselves against the Crown's might. While the southern colonies maintained primarily an agricultural economy, based on slave labor and with practically no industrial assets, those in the North did have a few manufactories capable of producing armaments and other war matériel. Still, they were no match for the industrialization that had transformed Great Britain into the world's most powerful nation.

As debate continued, reports reached Congress that a joint force of colonial militiamen under the command of Ethan Allen, leader of an irregular force known as the Green Mountain Boys, and Benedict Arnold, a colonel in the Massachusetts militia, had stormed and seized Ticonderoga, the British fortress situated on the shore of Lake Champlain, as well as the fortification at nearby Crown Point. Congressional members were heartened by the victory but realized that when the news reached London, a more aggressive stand toward the colonies would most likely be adopted by Parliament.

On the last day of May, Washington wrote to his friend George Fairfax, now living in England, revealing his growing animosity toward Great Britain. "Unhappy it is though to reflect," he declared, "that a Brother's Sword has been sheathed in a Brother's breast, and that, the once happy and peaceful plains of America are either to be drenched with Blood, or Inhabited by Slaves. Sad alternative! But can a virtuous Man hesitate in his choice?"

Discussion in Congress inevitably turned toward the formation of a continental army made up of militiamen from all the colonies. Names of potential leaders of the force were also suggested, particularly those of Artemas Ward, commander of the Massachusetts militia, and Charles Lee, a former British officer and soldier of fortune. But John Adams had other ideas for the role. Since all hostile action so far had occurred in Massachusetts and New York, involving militia primarily from the northern colonies, why not appoint a southerner as the commander in chief, thus providing a balance of power? And who from the South was a more likely candidate than George Washington, a French and Indian War veteran, commander of the Virginia militia, and an outspoken critic of the Crown?

On June 14, 1775, Washington wrote in his diary that he "Dined at Mr. Saml. Merediths" and "Spent the Evening at home." On the fifteenth, he recorded that he "Dined at Burn's in the Field. Spent the Eveng. On a Committee." He did not allude to the fact that on the fourteenth, John Adams had placed his name before Congress as a candidate to lead the Continental Army, nor that on the following day, he was unanimously elected to the post by his peers.

He had not asked for the assignment, nor pursued it. He attended most of the meetings of the second Congress dressed in the uniform of his Fairfax County Independent Company to demonstrate to his associates that Virginians were ready to fight for their liberties. And in order not to intimidate the other delegates and to allow them every freedom to discuss his qualifications openly and candidly, he had left the meeting chambers on the day of his nomination and did not attend the next day's sessions during the voting. His selection should have surprised no one, however, given his military background, his popularity not only in Virginia but in the other colonies as well, and his powerful presence. On the day of his acceptance, June 16, he humbly announced to the delegates, "With the utmost sincerity, I do not think my-self equal to the Command I am honored with," and informed them that he would fulfill his commission with no salary.

Washington delayed two days before writing to Martha that he had been appointed commander of the army. Almost apologetically, he told her that he had "used every endeavor in my power to avoid [it]" and that he had much rather spend his future with her than with the army. "Summon your whole fortitude," he implored her, "and pass your time as agreeably as possible." He confided that the appointment, in his judgment at least, was "destiny" and hoped that it was "designed to answer some good purpose."

Then he plunged himself into the business at hand. Congress had been busy with many matters in addition to appointing him commander of the army. It had authorized a colonial currency in the amount of two million dollars to pay expenses for the upcoming conflict. It had approved the formation of a fifteen-thousand-man standing army, to be increased as more British troops were sent to America. And it had appointed Artemas Ward, Israel Putnam, Charles Lee, and Philip John Schuyler to the rank of major general. Horatio Gates was made adjutant general. The five men were well qualified, all possessing a variety of military experience and all having served in the French and Indian War.

Of primary concern to the new commander were the arrangements he had to make for Martha's well-being during his absence. He wrote his errant son, Jack, suggesting that he and his wife move their home to Mount Vernon to provide companionship for her. He dispatched a letter to his brother, John Augustine, in which he hoped that friends would "visit & endeavor to keep up the spirits of my Wife," and wished that "you & my sister (although the distance is great) will find as much leisure this Summer, as to spend a little time at Mount Vernon." And to Martha, on June 23, as he was about to depart Philadelphia for his first assignment in Boston, he declared his "unalterable affection . . . which neither time or distance can change."

On the day after he accepted his commission in Philadelphia, British troops occupying Boston attacked colonial gun emplacements on Breed's Hill, located just north of town, on Charlestown peninsula. During the previous twenty-four hours, the ill-trained American army had placed the fortifications on Breed's Hill rather than the higher and more defensible Bunker Hill nearby. The redcoats, hampered by their burdensome field packs and required to march in their unalterable, classic battle formation, were twice driven back with heavy losses before finally overwhelming the Americans when they ran out of ammunition. On the third sortie, the Yankees retreated, leaving the peninsula in the permanent possession of the British.

Washington's first mission was to proceed to Boston, assume command of the Massachusetts militia, and drive the British from the region. He left Philadelphia with Generals Schuyler and Lee on June 23 and learned of the battle at Breed's Hill while passing through New York City. Leaving Schuyler in charge, he arrived in Boston on Sunday, July 2, and after relieving General Ward, proceeded to establish headquarters in a nearby Cambridge mansion.

Two days later, the new commander issued his first general orders, calling for inventories of all available ordnance, equipment, and supplies, and officially announcing the promotions of Generals Ward, Lee, Schuyler, and Putnam. He proclaimed that all colonial troops were now joined together under authority of the "United Provinces of North America" and cautioned that "all Distinctions of Colonies . . . be laid aside; so that one and the same Spirit may animate the whole, and the only Contest be, who shall render . . . the most essential service to the Great and common cause in which we are all engaged." He admonished all officers to be sure their men were neat and clean at all times and that they had straw for bedding. He also outlawed fishing in nearby freshwater ponds for fear that the men would contract smallpox, and he prohibited the firing of arms and cannons in camp.

Soon after his arrival in Cambridge, Washington learned that a number of American soldiers had been captured by the British and treated like common criminals with no regard for their health and sanitary needs. He immediately dispatched a letter to the Crown's commander, General Thomas Gage, declaring, "The Rights of Humanity . . . are universally binding." He added that he "hoped [the Crown] would have dictated a more tender Treatment of those Individuals, whom Chance or War had put in your Power." In closing, he promised that if the British treated American prisoners with kindness and care, he would reciprocate, but that if they continued to mistreat his men, then captured redcoats "will feel its Effects" and be governed by "exactly . . . the Rule you . . . observe towards those of ours, now in your Custody."

Now he would wait. The British were well entrenched in Boston and around Breed's and Bunker Hills and showed no signs of evacuating. Although he estimated American troop strength at around sixteen thousand to Britain's twelve thousand, Washington quickly discovered that his men were "in a very insecure state" and that much work had to be done to condition them into a cohesive and effective fighting force. Supply returns revealed that he had access to only ninety barrels of powder, enough for eight rounds per soldier with none to spare for the cannons. He pleaded with the Continental Congress, still meeting in Philadelphia, to replenish his powder and lead supplies as rapidly as possible and, in a letter to the governor of Rhode Island, he even endorsed a daring raid on Bermuda, where large stores of powder existed. He declared, "We are in a Situation which requires us to run all Risques. No danger is to be considered."

With cool weather approaching, the Continental staff faced the dilemma of feeding, housing, and properly clothing the army during the New England winter. The shrinking size of the militia compounded problems as growing numbers of soldiers elected not to reenlist and troop strength fell to less than ten thousand. Hoping to end the conflict before the arrival of winter and the loss of additional manpower, Washington recommended to his three division commanders—Lee, Putnam, and Ward—that they immediately engage the British at Boston, but extended discussions and a further analysis of the proposal persuaded him to postpone the attack.

Reviewing progress at the end of his first six months as commander in chief, Washington was saddened, but also encouraged. That his ragtag army had serious problems, no one could deny. But progress was being made, and if the Continental Congress would only demonstrate some sign of solidarity among the diverse colonies and provide the support he needed, he was convinced America could win the war.

"We Are Determined to Shake Off All Connexions with a State So Unjust"

As the fall and early winter of 1775 progressed, Washington and his staff spent most of their time providing advanced training to the militia, wrestling with the manpower and reenlistment problems, and strengthening the line of fortifications around Boston. The town was situated on a near-island and was connected with the mainland by a narrow spit of ground that was heavily fortified by British troops, making any advance by the Americans nearly impossible. Washington's three top generals—Putnam, Lee, and Ward—commanded the center, left, and right wings of the Continental fortifications, a line that ran west of Boston for around eight miles and connected the Mystic River in the north with Dorchester Heights in the south. Boston Harbor, east of town, was filled with British warships awaiting orders from General Sir William Howe, a member of Parliament and the new commander in chief of the British army, who had succeeded Thomas Gage in October.

By now, Washington firmly advocated American independence, not mere accommodation with the Crown, and the rock-solid respect he once held toward Great Britain had crumbled. A proclamation by King George III declaring that Americans were on the brink of rebellion and calling upon all officers and men of the army to suppress the uprising prompted the Virginian to confide to a friend, "The spirit of freedom beat[s] too high in us to submit to slavery. . . . We are determined to shake off all connexions with a state so unjust and unnatural."

To protect New York and New England from a possible British invasion from Canada, members of the Second Continental Congress had agreed early in their session to dispatch forces led by General Schuyler and his second-in-command, Brigadier General Richard Montgomery, an Irish-born New Yorker, to occupy Montreal. Some months later, in September 1775, Washington ordered Colonel Benedict Arnold and one thousand colonial troops to capture Quebec. For weeks no news had been received from either commander, but as December came to a close, word finally arrived in Cambridge that Montgomery, in command after Schuyler fell ill, had indeed attacked Montreal, successfully occupying it on November 13, after fierce fighting. Two nearby British forts, Chambly and St. Johns, had also been seized. Although news would not reach Washington until sometime later, Benedict Arnold and his army had not fared as well. Arnold's force, having meanwhile been joined by Montgomery's men, had attacked Quebec on December 31, but the assault failed. Montgomery was killed in action, and Arnold was severely wounded.

While awaiting news from the Canadian campaign, Washington ordered General Henry Knox, a former bookseller and participant in the Boston Massacre, to inventory, commandeer, and deliver to Cambridge every piece of artillery he could find, particularly the cannons captured by Allen and Arnold at Fort Ticonderoga the previous May. Knox and his command braved ice and subzero weather, hauling the heavy equipment through the wilderness to present to their commander. The ordnance provided the missing link for Washington's long-planned attack on Boston.

Although General Gage had been the Crown's commander in chief during the British charge up Breed's Hill the previous June, it was William Howe who actually led the troops, and he bore several wounds to prove it. Following Gage's recall to London, Howe assumed command and supervised the further strengthening of the Boston defenses in case the Americans tried to reoccupy the town. As the spring of 1776 approached, he was satisfied that the results of his efforts would fend off any colonial attack.

On Monday evening, March 4, Washington quietly dispatched all of the newly acquired artillery, along with two thousand troops, to occupy Dorchester Heights, situated on a peninsula south of Boston and overlooking the town. He had replenished his powder supply and, hoping to distract the British from the nighttime maneuver, he ordered his remaining cannoneers to bombard

Boston with continuous, blistering artillery fire. On Tuesday morning, Howe discovered that the cannonade plaguing his army throughout the night was the least of his troubles. Now, across a narrow stretch of water to the south, three hundred additional guns and hundreds of artillerymen stared down upon his command.

Washington theorized that when the British discovered they were in such a vulnerable position, Howe would dispatch a force across the water to Dorchester Heights to rout the American artillery; then, according to his plan, elements of the colonial army numbering around four thousand would invade Boston from the west, even as the British were departing town from the south. During the early afternoon, Howe's initial force of one thousand redcoats boarded six transport boats and started across the water, immediately encountering trouble as the fickle tide swept them eastward into Boston Harbor and away from their intended landing site. Meanwhile, a terrible storm arose that forced both Howe and Washington to scrap their plans.

The British troops returned to Boston, and Washington wrote in a letter to a friend, "Whether from an apprehension that our works are now too formidable to make any impression on, or from what other causes I know not, but their hostile appearances have subsided." Over the next few days, he and his staff watched in amazement as the frantic British army evacuated Boston aboard the tall ships of the Royal Navy moored in the harbor. On March 19, Washington sent a letter to John Hancock, president of the Continental Congress, proudly proclaiming that, as of the previous Sunday, "Forces of the United Colonies are now in actual Possession [of Boston]." He congratulated Hancock and the Congress on the occasion, "particularly as it was effected without endangering the Lives and property of the remaining unhappy Inhabitants."

Upon entering Boston, Washington discovered that, in their haste, Howe's forces had left behind a large number of cannons and a huge mortar, along with other war matériel valued at over twenty-five thousand pounds sterling. He found the town "not in so bad a state as I expected to find it," although he was met by many resident loyalists who had either refused to leave their homes or else were unable to find space on the departing British ships. Washington wrote, "One or two of them [loyalists] have done what a great many of them ought to have done long ago, committed suicide." Then, demonstrating the kindness that he extended to friend and foe through his life, he added, "Would it not be good policy to grant a generous amnesty, to conquer these people by a generous forgiveness?"

The British fleet carrying Howe's entire army did not sail far, however, mooring in the outer harbor until March 27. Fearing that the rapid departure might be a trick, Washington maintained most of this troop strength in the area until he was certain the evacuation was real. Then, determining that his next encounter with Howe would occur in New York, he dispatched five regiments and a rifle battalion there. On April 4, after the fleet finally set sail eastward, eventually to Nova Scotia for refitting, Washington, with most of his remaining army, departed for New York, leaving General Ward in command of Boston.

MARTHA WASHINGTON

Martha Washington visited the army's Cambridge headquarters in late 1775 and brought new life to the Americans. The attack on Boston had been delayed until the following spring, and the men were relegated to sitting out the long, cold New England winter in camp. Martha's appearance provided the general with one of the few bright moments in his hurried life, and her visit that first year of his military campaign began a tradition that she maintained for the duration of the war.

Mrs. Washington, born Martha Dandridge on June 21, 1731, in New Kent County, Virginia, was the daughter of John Dandridge, the wealthy master of a large plantation located on the Pamunkey River, and Frances Jones Dandridge. Martha was privileged with all of the finer aspects of life, and she married Daniel Parke Custis when she was eighteen. The couple eventually had four children, two of whom died as infants. One year after her husband's untimely death, she married George Washington.

She steadfastly supported all his endeavors: gentleman farmer, Virginia burgess, commander in chief of the Continental Army, and the nation's first president. When, in 1774–75, the future of the American colonies lay in doubt and her husband was criticized by one of her loyalist friends for his strong anti-British views, she replied, "Yes, I foresee consequences—dark days, domestic happiness suspended, social enjoyments abandoned, and eternal separations on earth possible. But my mind is made up, my heart is in the cause. George is right; he is always right."

Martha was described by camp followers as "rather plump, but fresh and of an agreeable countenance." When visiting with the army, she dressed plainly, showing no sign of her great wealth and affluence. She often organized the other women in camp into social clubs, whose members spent their time sewing and knitting. Whenever the subject of her husband was brought up, she gleefully referred to him as "the Old Man."

After Washington was elected president, Martha served as the first First Lady with the same grace and good taste that she had demonstrated at Mount Vernon. She hosted visitors at the Executive Mansion in New York City, and later in Philadelphia, with customary charm and politeness and treated all visitors as if they were family. A guest in 1794 described her as "extremely simple in dress," wearing "her gray hair turned up under a very plain cap."

Martha Washington survived her husband by only twenty-nine months, and when she died on May 22, 1802, at age seventy, she was laid to rest beside "the Old Man" in the family crypt at Mount Vernon.

"Good God! Have I Got Such Troops as These?"

embers of Congress were heartened when news reached them in Philadelphia that the British had evacuated Boston. Continental troops had yet to make physical contact with the Crown's army, and proof of the Americans' competence could be demonstrated only when the real fighting began. But leaders felt confident that their choice of George Washington as commander in chief was the correct one and that he would prevail. Now, as the summer of 1776 approached, other important matters had to be resolved.

The delegates knew that Americans stood sharply divided in their attitudes toward Great Britain. One faction, although displeased by the mother country's recent treatment of the colonies, nevertheless maintained an intense loyalty to the Crown. The opposition envisioned no other alternative to the declining relationship but to sue—or to fight—for total independence. By May, in fact, Rhode Island had already declared its sovereignty, while delegates from Virginia, Massachusetts, and several other colonies had been instructed by officials at home to urge Congress to sever relations with England.

In Virginia, one of the most vocal colonies for immediate and total independence, George Mason, Washington's close friend and neighbor, penned a "Declaration of Rights" that was approved on June 12. Less than three weeks later, Virginia adopted its first constitution, which declared, "The government of this country, as formerly exercised under the Crown of Great Britain, is *totally dissolved*." In the meantime, Congress had charged another Virginian, thirty-three-year-old Thomas Jefferson, with the responsibility of preparing a draft of a Declaration of Independence for consideration by its members.

Jefferson presented the document to delegates on June 28, 1776, and it was approved on July 4. Initially, only Hancock and Charles Thomson, the president and secretary of Congress, signed it, keeping secret the names of the others who sanctioned it, for fear of British reprisals should independence not actually be won (the remaining delegates signed on August 2). On July 6, the Declaration was published for the first time in *The Philadelphia Evening Post*, and two days later it was read in public to a crowd of Philadelphia residents. It left no doubt which path Americans would take: "These United Colonies are, and of Right ought to be Free and Independent States; that they are Absolved from all Allegiance to the British Crown, and that all political connection between them and the State of Great Britain is and ought to be totally dissolved. . . ."

Washington learned of Congress's action on July 9, in New York City, and announced to his men in the general orders of the same day that, "impelled by the dictates of duty, policy and necessity," the colonies had cut their ties with Great Britain. He further stated that at six o'clock on the ninth, at general muster, the Declaration would be read and discussed, thereby "showing the grounds & reasons for this measure."

Washington and most of his army had arrived in New York from Boston on April 13, convinced that America's second-largest city would be General Howe's next target. Situated on the southern tip of Manhattan Island, at the junction of the Hudson and East Rivers, the town was conveniently accessible by water, through Long Island Sound from the northeast or the Atlantic Ocean from the east, and it provided excellent docking facilities for large ships. The majority of the nineteen-thousand-man army occupied Brooklyn Heights, on the western end of Long Island, directly across the East River from New York City. Washington ordered old vessel hulls and other obstructions to be sunk at the river's mouth to hinder British ships from entering and, to further fortify the area, he instructed his cannoneers to build artillery emplacements on both sides of the stream's mouth.

While awaiting Howe's appearance, the Virginian traveled to Philadelphia, where he implored Congress to resolve the army's dwindling manpower problem by creating a more permanent and professional fighting force. Colonial militias invariably fell short of their enlistment quotas, and the men who did volunteer fully expected to return to their homes in two or three months, especially when harvest time neared. What was needed, he said, was a much-enlarged, better-equipped regular army of men who would serve for years. "To bring Men to a proper degree of Subordination, is not the work of a day, a Month or even a year," he wrote.

Complicating affairs as he was pleading with Congress, Washington learned that England had negotiated with the heads of several German states and hired about ten thousand mercenaries, the majority Hessians named after the Electorate of Hesse. Many of them were already aboard ships crossing the Atlantic. In May, still in Philadelphia and much concerned about the future, he wrote to his brother, "We expect a very bloody Summer of it in New York . . . as it is there I expect the grand efforts of the Enemy will be aim'd."

The British fleet that Washington had watched sail away from Boston in April arrived offshore in New York on June 29. As the ships dropped anchor in the harbor, ten thousand soldiers disembarked on Staten Island and pitched camp. Admiral Richard Howe, older brother of General Howe and, ironically, a longtime sympathizer of the American cause, soon arrived from England with more ships, more redcoats, and the first of the Hessians. By late summer, the Crown's presence in the New York area totaled some thirty thousand soldiers and scores of naval craft.

On August 22, General Howe landed fifteen thousand troops on Long Island and prepared to assail the American fortifications perched on Brooklyn Heights. Five days later, and before Washington's "panicky, green defenders," as historian Ralph K. Andrist called them, realized it, the redcoats had outflanked them and driven the patriots to the banks of the East River. In the chaos following the collapse of the American lines, Howe, for some unexplained reason, broke off the fight and allowed the Continentals to escape across the river, but not before "whole Regiments . . . half ones & . . . Companies at a time" deserted, Washington wrote. His casualties were sizable, 1,400, out of a force of 9,000, but most of the supplies, equipment, and other matériel were saved in the retreat, orchestrated by Washington himself, who stayed in the saddle for forty-eight continuous hours, issuing commands.

The debacle gave him yet another occasion to voice his dismal opinion of the army. He wrote to John Hancock, "All these circumstances fully confirm the opinion I ever entertained and which I more than once in my letters took the liberty of mentioning to Congress, that no dependence could be put in a Militia or other Troops than those enlisted and embodied for a longer period than our regulations heretofore have prescribed." He ended the letter by suggesting that perhaps bounties in the form of land grants could be awarded to long-serving veterans.

Washington requested that his troops be allowed to burn New York City, now in an extremely vulnerable situation. Congress refused, ordering him instead to defend it "at all costs." Assuming that a new attack by Howe was imminent, the general split his army, sending half of it to Harlem Heights, located along the Hudson River in the northwest corner of Manhattan Island, and dividing the other half between the garrison in New York City and the forested expanse that lay between it and the Heights.

On September 15, Howe struck at a point along the East River about four miles north of the city. Thousands of redcoats and Hessians streamed ashore from eighty-four barges, protected by the big guns aboard the warships anchored in the river. The Americans were terrified, and scores fled past Washington as he observed the retreat in "surprise and mortification." He was livid, dashed his hat to the ground, and rode after the frightened soldiers, ordering them to return to their positions. "Are these the men with whom I am to defend America? Good God! Have I got such troops as these?" he shouted.

Most of the American army, including the garrison at New York City and the elements scattered between the town and Harlem Heights, now regrouped at the Heights. On the sixteenth, as the opposing forces again faced each other nearby, Washington watched in amazement as his militia fought with clockwork precision, driving the British in retreat toward the East River. The skirmish represented his first combat victory over Howe, but he knew he was still badly outnumbered and outgunned. As the British fell back on New York City to reorganize their battalions and lay plans for the occupation of Manhattan Island and the surrounding region, Washington and his staff conferred at Harlem Heights.

Four weeks later, several British ships carrying sixteen thousand redcoats and Hessians sailed up the East River into Long Island Sound and beyond the northern tip of Manhattan Island. Alarmed that Howe would march westward, thereby severing the American army from New England, Washington and part of his command departed for White Plains, twelve miles to the northeast. Failure to contain the British there drove the Americans across the Hudson River and into New Jersey while Howe's army returned southward and overran Fort Washington, near Harlem Heights on the east side of the river. With the fall of the fort, the Continental Army lost two thousand soldiers, as well as artillery and supplies. Washington, his army decimated, retreated sixty miles southwestward through New Jersey to the Delaware River, which he crossed as he entered Pennsylvania in early December.

On December 10, as he awaited reinforcements, Washington wrote to a cousin, "I wish to Heaven it was in my power to give you a more favorable account of our situation than it is." He said troop strength was down to around five thousand, not sufficient to defend Philadelphia if Howe decided to attack. To his brother eight days later, after learning that Congress had fled Philadelphia to reconvene in Baltimore, he wrote, "I think the game is pretty near up, owing . . . principally to the accursed policy of short Inlistments, and placing too great a dependence on the Militia the Evil consequences of which were foretold 15 months ago."

In the December 23, 1776, issue of *The Pennsylvania Journal,* a popular Philadelphia newspaper, Thomas Paine—a thirty-nine-year-old transplanted Englishman who earlier in the year had published the popular book *Common Sense,* which strongly advocated American independence—contributed an essay entitled "The Crisis." It opened:

> These are the times that try men's souls. The summer soldier and the sunshine patriot will, in this crisis, shrink from the service of their country; but he that stands it *now,* deserves the love and thanks of man and woman. Tyranny, like hell, is not easily conquered; yet we have this consolation with us, that the harder the conflict, the more glorious the triumph.

History has failed to record whether Washington read Paine's philosophical words at the time they were first published. If he did, he would have agreed that the times were indeed trying; whether or not, at this low ebb in his military career, he placed much stock in the glory of his ultimate triumph is doubtful.

"I Am Now Convinced . . . This Army Must . . . Starve, Dissolve, or Disperse"

Desperately worried about the dwindling of his armed forces and the dismal chances of receiving sufficient replacements, Washington labored through most of December 1776 in a state of depression. He had commanded the Continental Army for eighteen months, and the only real combat success he had achieved was the feeble victory over Howe's troops at Harlem Heights. Unless Congress rectified the manpower problem by establishing an army of full-time soldiers, enlisted for terms of two or three years, the newly formed United Colonies might as well admit that their fight for independence was lost.

When it seemed that affairs could get no worse, Washington learned that three elite Hessian regiments and one troop of British light cavalry were encamped across the Delaware River, nine miles away in Trenton, New Jersey. Although most of Howe's army had retired to winter quarters on Manhattan and Staten Islands, the

British commander had established several outposts in the field, one of which was the small garrison at Trenton.

Washington formulated a plan whereby he and his troops would break camp at dusk on Christmas evening, calculating that they could cross the river by midnight and have plenty of time to make the short march to Trenton for an attack at daybreak. Bitter cold, ice floes in the river, and an impending storm, however, significantly delayed the army's arrival on the far shore. As the cross-country trek to Trenton began, the storm, with its powerful winds and heavy sleet and snow, struck with a fury, causing horses, men, and artillery caissons to slip and slide all over the roadway. Miraculously, when the Americans reached the outskirts of town at around eight o'clock, the Hessians, most still suffering from the effects of their Christmas revelry, had not yet arisen.

The encounter was over within minutes. Washington's 2,400 troops descended upon the town and its 1,500 defenders with fervor, capturing nearly nine hundred Germans and killing or wounding forty more. Several cannons, a large supply of small arms and ammunition, and four enemy regimental flags were also seized. No Americans were killed and only four were wounded. On the following day, Washington wrote to the Congress, proudly reporting the victory and the conduct of his troops: "In justice to the officers and men, I must add, that their behaviour upon this occasion, reflects the highest honor upon them . . . [and] when it came to the charge, each seemed to vie with the other in pressing forward, and were I to give a preference to any particular corps, I should do great injustice to the others."

Between Christmas and the end of the year, encouraged by their victory, about half of Washington's troops reenlisted, following an impassioned speech from their commander in which he declared, "You have done all I asked you to do, and more than could be reasonably expected, but your country is at stake: your wives, your houses, and all that you hold dear. . . . The present is emphatically the crisis which is to decide our destiny."

One week after the confrontation at Trenton, the Americans were further buoyed when they scored a second coup against Howe. An enlarged British force under the command of General Charles Cornwallis, a veteran of the Seven Years' War, had been dispatched by Howe and had traveled southward from New York to retake the town. On January 2, 1777, near the village of Princeton, located twelve miles north of Trenton, the Americans encountered two enemy regiments en route to join Cornwallis. That night, Washington ordered his men to keep the campfires burning while he marched most of his army behind enemy lines. The next morning the British, who had been lulled into believing the patriots were sleeping, were shocked to find their own camp encircled. At Princeton, later in the day, a spirited skirmish followed in which Washington, mounted on his white horse, gallantly led the charge, calling out, "It's a fine fox chase, my boys!" Before Cornwallis arrived with the rest of the army, Washington's force, with nearly three hundred prisoners, sped even farther north to Morristown, where winter quarters were established.

For the most part, winter camp was uneventful. Washington alternated his time between skirmishing with the British and reenergizing the troops. He cajoled Congress, now back in Philadelphia, to authorize additional matériel for his exhausted army. Frequent pleas for assistance annoyed many delegates and one, Robert Morris, retorted that if the general presented "the best side of the picture" occasionally, he might receive a better response from the legislators. On January 25, Washington issued a proclamation ordering all persons who had declared allegiance to Great Britain to report to the nearest Continental Army establishment, denounce all previous vows, surrender all documents of protection, and take the oath of allegiance to the United States. Otherwise, he wrote, they would be "treated as common enemies of the American States." And, from Mount Vernon, Martha arrived in March for a two-month visit, bringing with her welcome news from home, family, and friends.

During the summer, rumors reached Morristown that General Howe, who had only recently broken winter camp, belatedly planned to move up the Hudson River and rendezvous with General John Burgoyne, another veteran of the Seven Years' War and the recent captor of Fort Ticonderoga. In a pincer movement, they would close the Hudson to the Americans and isolate New England from the rest of the colonies. In reality, however, no one knew Howe's exact location or his plans. "I cannot give you any certain account of Genl. Howe's intended Operations," lamented Washington to General Philip Schuyler. "His conduct is puzzling and embarrassing, beyond measure. . . . At one time the Ships are standing up towards the North River. In a little while they are going up the Sound, and in an Hour after they are going out of the Hook."

While Washington awaited news of Howe, nineteen-year-old Marie Joseph Paul Yves Roch Gilbert du Motier, marquis de Lafayette, a French nobleman who had forsaken family and fortune to offer his services to the American cause, arrived at headquarters. In years to come, Washington treated him as a son, and the marquis's contributions to the war effort would prove inestimable. Unlike Lafayette, several other Frenchmen failed to impress Washington when they interviewed for assignments in the army. Of them, he protested to Congress, "You cannot conceive what a weight these kind of people are upon the Service, and upon me in particular, few of them have any knowledge of the Branches which they profess to understand, and those that have, are entirely useless as officers from their ignorance of the English language."

On July 24, Howe made his initial move to occupy Philadelphia, dispatching 220 ships and fifteen thousand men from New York City to the mouth of Chesapeake Bay. The armada ascended the bay and, on August 25, the troops disembarked near Elkton, Maryland, only forty miles from their destination. At Morristown, Washington quickly assembled his army, now increased to nearly eleven thousand by the successful reenlistment campaign, and marched southwestward toward the capital. He soon arrived at Brandywine creek, west of Philadelphia, establishing his defenses between town and the oncoming redcoats. On September 11, Washington engaged them near Chad's Ford. His failure to check the British force, partially due to fauly intelligence, was reminiscent of the earlier affair at Brooklyn Heights, when his opponents swept around the American lines and routed his soldiers from their positions.

From nearby Chester, at midnight on the day of the battle, Washington wrote to John Hancock, "We have been obliged to leave the enemy masters of the field." Fortunately, he reported, losses had been minimal, although eight cannons were captured and Lafayette and several other officers were wounded. He advised, however, "I am happy to find the troops in good spirits; and I hope another time we shall compensate for the losses now sustained." Meantime, in late September, Lord Cornwallis occupied Philadelphia, and the Continental Congress fled once again, reconvening later in the month in York, Pennsylvania.

On October 4, Washington made one final attempt before winter to engage the British army. Near the village of Germantown, on the outskirts of Philadelphia, he gathered his army for the attack. During the opening moments of the encounter, he was greatly heartened when he observed hundreds of enemy troops retire before the onslaught of the Americans. As he led his soldiers past a palatial mansion called the Chew House, however, they were met with vicious small-arms fire coming from the building's windows. Cannon fire failed to dislodge the house's defenders, and Washington left a small detachment of riflemen to deal with the situation while the main army followed him in pursuit of the still-retreating redcoats.

He could smell victory. How wonderful it would be to defeat the British then and there and force them to evacuate Philadelphia. Envisioning the enemy's total rout, the general soon collected his senses when he observed part of his advance troops suddenly bolt after running out of ammunition. Panic-stricken, they had begun a retreat of their own.

A monumental, decisive win over the British that he so yearned for once again eluded him. It remained for one of his compatriots, General Horatio Gates, to effect the first large-scale American victory of the war in defeating General Burgoyne at Saratoga, along the upper Hudson River, on October 17, and forcing the surrender of 5,700 redcoats. Disappointed that it was not he who had triumphed, Washington was nevertheless proud of his associate, writing to Gates on October 30, "I do myself the pleasure to congratulate you on the signal success of the Army under your command, in compelling Genl. Burgoyne and his whole force, to surrender themselves prisoners of War."

After skirmishing with the Americans, the British returned to Philadelphia, where they would bivouac for the winter. In late December, Washington selected a site called Valley Forge, twenty miles northwest of the capital, for his winter quarters. From there, the melancholy general wrote Congress on the twenty-third, "I am now convinced, beyond a doubt, that unless some great . . . change suddenly takes place . . . this Army must inevitably be reduced to one or the other of these three things; starve, dissolve or disperse in order to obtain subsistence in the best manner they can."

Washington also had other matters on his mind, among which were rumors that his position as commanding general might be in jeopardy.

"My Temper Leads Me to Peace and Harmony with All Men"

Confident that the forthcoming winter at Valley Forge would be harsh and unforgiving for his battered, hungry army, General Washington began requisitioning badly needed food and fodder for the men and animals. On December 20, the day of his arrival, he ordered all residents within a seventy-mile radius of headquarters to thresh their grain promptly or risk its confiscation. Three days later he was shocked to learn that his commissary department had only twenty-five barrels of flour and no meat with which to feed the eleven-thousand-man army. On the same day, he reported that nearly three thousand troops were unfit for duty due to lack of food and warm clothing.

He was still wrestling with the food problem two months later, when he reminded his three supply officers that the men had received no meat rations in four days. "The troops must have instant relief," he said, "or we shall have reason to apprehend the worst consequences. . . . I need not mention to you the necessity of secrecy in an affair of such delicacy." Clearly, he feared a mutiny.

Washington had already issued detailed guidelines for building the log huts that would house his troops in the coming months. Each structure was to measure fourteen by sixteen feet and accommodate a fireplace in the rear and a door in the side facing the street. Generals would receive a private hut, but other officers and enlisted men were to share. The construction took nearly a month to complete, but not until all of his men were sheltered did Washington move from his own hut into a nearby stone farmhouse that he would used as his private billet as well as his army headquarters.

The winter of 1777–78 was one of the harshest on record. From December well into March, the American army endured the frigid weather as food and medical supplies dwindled with no relief in sight. Dr. Albigence Waldo, the surgeon for a Connecticut infantry regiment, left a poignant recollection of the demanding times:

> Poor food—hard lodging—cold weather—fatigue—nasty clothes—nasty cookery—vomit half my time—smoked out of my senses—the devil's in it—I can't endure it. . . . A pox on my luck. There comes a bowl of beef-soup—full of burnt leaves and dirt, sickish enough to make a Hector spew—away with it boys—I'll live like a chameleon upon air. . . . There comes a soldier, his bare feet are seen through his worn-out shoes, his legs nearly naked from the tattered remains of an only pair of stockings, his breeches not sufficient to cover his nakedness, his shirt hanging in

strings; his hair disheveled; his face meager. . . . He comes and cries with an air of wretchedness and despair, "I am sick, my feet lame, my legs sore, my body covered with this tormenting itch . . . and all the reward I shall get will be— 'Poor Will is dead!' "

If the weeks of starvation, deprivation, and death at Valley Forge were not sufficient to discourage Washington, he faced another, equally serious issue. During the previous fall, when General Horatio Gates notified him of Burgoyne's defeat at Saratoga, Gates had entrusted the victory message to one of his staff, twenty-year-old Colonel James Wilkinson of Maryland. On his way to report to the commander in chief, the young colonel spent an evening at a tavern in which a few of Washington's officers were guests. Too much drink loosened Wilkinson's tongue, and he confided to the others that Gates had recently received a letter from Washington's inspector general, Thomas Conway—an Irish-born Frenchman who liked to brag that he had once served under Frederick the Great—in which the patronizing Conway wrote, "Heaven has been determined to save your Country, or a weak General and bad Councillors would have ruined it."

Washington perceived the information in the letter to be critical of his abilities as a commander. It came as no surprise that he had enemies both in the army and in Congress—those who preferred his replacement by someone else, perhaps General Gates or even the British veteran General Charles Lee, who had always boasted of being the most experienced officer in the American army. But, such an overt condemnation by members of his own staff troubled him and suggested that a much wider conspiracy existed. In the affair that became known as the Conway Cabal, he wrote to Gates on January 4, 1778, and chastised him, prompting Gates to deny knowledge of the incident. A lengthy exchange of letters between the two generals ensued, and Washington, wanting to put the entire matter to rest, finally accepted Gates's denial. In late February he wrote his final word on the matter: "My temper leads me to peace and harmony with all men; and it is peculiarly my wish, to avoid any personal feuds or dissentions with those, who are embarked in the same great national interest with myself." Conway quickly lost support, even friendship, among his plotting associates and eventually submitted to involuntary retirement.

After relief finally arrived at Valley Forge in early March 1778, by what Washington called "the exertions of our Friends in different quarters," the army, from a provisions standpoint at least, stood on more solid footing. Stores of food and clothing, still not plentiful, were sufficient to carry the troops through the remainder of the winter and into spring. As fair weather approached, the commander turned his attentions to training. Early in the war he realized that the army suffered from two serious problems, and he frequently voiced his solutions to Congress whenever occasion arose. His first concern was the stability of the troops. Soldiers who enlisted for short terms—the militiamen furnished to him by the various states, for example—although they might exhibit bravery and patriotism, could not compete with their more permanent, professional counterparts. In a message to Congress he wrote:

> To place any dependance upon Militia, is, assuredly, resting upon a broken staff. Men just dragged from the tender Scenes of domestick life; unaccustomed to the din of Arms; totally unacquainted with every kind of Military skill, which being followed by a want of confidence in themselves, when opposed to Troops regularly train'd, disciplined, and appointed, superior in knowledge, and superior in Arms, makes them timid, and ready to fly from their own shadows.

Congress finally agreed to his logic in September 1776, when delegates voted to raise a standing army of 110 battalions totaling seventy-six thousand men. In reality, this ambitious figure was never approached and Washington's army rarely numbered more than seventeen thousand able-bodied soldiers at any given time.

While he continued his pleas from Valley Forge, there came a solution to another nagging problem, the army's lack of proper instruction in the art, tactics, and logistics of warfare. Just as breaking weather permitted outdoor activity to begin, Congress assigned Friedrich Wilhelm Ludolf Gerhard Augustin, baron von Steuben, a forty-seven-year-old Prussian army veteran, to the commander's staff. Von Steuben's specialty was training, and he was charged with developing the uninformed patriots into a disciplined, dependable force that, when winter camp broke, could successfully face the might of the British army.

Although Von Steuben spoke no English, he proved to be an excellent drillmaster. He quickly understood that the patriots differed greatly from the uneducated masses who comprised the armies of Europe. These were enthusiastic, intelligent men who wanted to learn and whose abilities had been hindered only by their lack of training and discipline. Comparing the average American soldier with his counterpart in France, Austria, or Prussia, he confided to a friend back home, "You say to your soldier, 'Do this,' and he doeth it, but I am obliged to say, 'This is the reason that you ought to do that,' and then he does it."

The Prussian organized the army into smaller, more easily controlled units and taught the troops the crafts of close-order drill, bayonet skirmishing, and battle formation. He combined the commonsense techniques of guerrilla fighting, in which the patriots already excelled, with the classic systems of European warfare. Building upon the merger of the two, he whipped his students into a precision fighting machine. For the eager Americans, training became a task to look forward to as each unit tried to outperform the others.

In May, as Von Steuben neared the end of the training cycle with his new charges and apprised Washington of the outstanding progress that the army had made, the commander in chief received more good news. The government of France, now convinced that the American quest for independence was not just a poorly organized gesture by a few malcontents, but rather the expression of the majority of concerned citizens, realized that a permanent break with Great Britain must occur. On the previous December 17, upon learning of Burgoyne's defeat at Saratoga, France officially recognized American independence and, three weeks later, the two countries signed treaties of alliance, amity, and commerce. When Washington heard the official news at Valley Forge in early May, he ordered the entire army to celebrate with the firing of artillery and a concerted cheer, "Long Live the King of France."

In an attempt to keep the Franco-American coalition from being consummated, Britain's prime minister, Lord North, earl of Guilford, sent to the Continental Congress, which was convened in York, Pennsylvania, a list of conciliatory measures, along with assurances that a peace commission would be established. North's proposals were rejected on June 17, 1778.

More news from England arrived in May. Lord North, displeased at Howe's progress with Washington and his upstart army, recalled the general, replacing him with Howe's second-in-command, General Sir Henry Clinton. This man, described by Washington biographer James Thomas Flexner as "dour, neurotic, [and] self-righteous," had as little respect for his superior as did the propagandist Thomas Paine, who wrote a facetious open letter to Howe, published in *The Crisis:* "You have moved in and out, backward and forward, round and round, as if valor consisted of a military jig. The history and figure of your movements would be truly ridiculous could they be justly delineated. They resemble the labors of a puppy pursuing its tail."

As soon as Clinton arrived in Philadelphia to assume command, he was ordered by London to evacuate the city.

"Unless Congress Speaks in a More Decisive Tone . . . Our Cause Is Lost"

With the worrisome days of the Conway Cabal behind him, and encouraged by France's entry into the war as well as his army's increased readiness, Washington prepared to break winter camp. Meantime, General Charles Lee had returned to headquarters following a period of British captivity, during which, unknown to Washington, he had become General Howe's confidant, providing critical intelligence to the enemy.

Washington became aware of Clinton's planned evacuation of Philadelphia from the camp's washerwomen, who had reported that the British troops in town were frantically preparing for what appeared to be an immediate departure. The withdrawal began at 10 A.M. on June 18, 1778, when several regiments, in all about ten thousand troops, crossed the Delaware River headed for New York City. Within four hours, the American army was in pursuit, and by the end of the day, the British line of march, burdened by 1,500 supply wagons, the artillery, and hundreds of camp followers, stretched for a dozen or more miles across the New Jersey countryside.

Lafayette, now promoted to major general, viewed the situation as perfectly suited for a massive American attack along the lumbering column and, with the support of other staff officers, urged immediate action. Lee, however, given to scoff at any strategy not his own, disagreed, publicly criticizing Washington and declaring him "not fit to command a sergeant's guard." Washington, out of respect for his old comrade, put the decision to a vote. The council of war, influenced by Lee's inflated reputation as a military tactician, elected not to attack. Later, Lafayette and other generals met with Washington and convinced him to override the decision and engage the enemy at once while it was still vulnerable.

Washington placed Lee, outraged by the overriding of the council's decision, in charge of a select five-thousand-man force, and, on the evening of June 27, his troops encamped six miles from the British rear guard, near Monmouth Court House, New Jersey. Washington ordered the attack for the following morning.

At 7 A.M. on a sweltering June 28, Lee's troops engaged the British. As Washington rode up from his camp three miles away, he heard distant artillery fire. Advancing, he was dumbfounded to see retreating Americans all around him, initially one or two individuals, then scores, then entire regiments. Upon finding Lee, Washington angrily demanded, "What is all this confusion for, and retreat?" Lee babbled a befuddled reply, placing blame on everything from faulty intelligence and imperfect terrain to his own reservations about whether the engagement should have ever taken place at all.

Washington was livid. He angrily dispatched Lee's confused troops to the rear to regroup and personally led fresh ones after the British, who watched in horror as the Americans, displaying the stern discipline taught them at Valley Forge by Von Steuben, raked them with artillery and small-arms fire until dusk, effectively delaying their retreat. It was not the victory Washington had hoped for, but it did prove to the British that the American army was now a force to contend with. Lafayette later extolled the commander in chief's cool response to the crisis, writing that he "seemed to arrest fortune with one glance. . . . His presence stopped the retreat. . . . His graceful bearing on horseback, his calm and deportment which still retained a trace of displeasure . . . were all calculated to inspire the highest degree of enthusiasm. . . . I thought . . . that I had never beheld so superb a man."

Although Washington's initial report to Congress describing the action at Monmouth omitted Lee's unconscionable actions on the field that day, a letter to his brother on July 4 was more direct: "When he [Lee] came up with the enemy, a retreat was commenced; whether by his own order, or from other causes, is now the subject of enquiry, & consequently improper to be discanted on, as he is in arrest, and a Court Martial sitting for trial of him." He added, "A Retreat however was the fact, be the causes as they may; and the disorder arising from it would have proved fatal to the Army."

Following Monmouth, Clinton retreated to New York, and Washington eventually retired his army for the winter to several locations across New Jersey and New York, establishing his headquarters in Middlebrook, situated twenty miles to the north of the battle site. Meanwhile, France, true to its promise to lend assistance to the United States, declared war on Great Britain in June 1778 and dispatched a squadron of frigates and twelve other armed ships, along with four thousand infantrymen to Philadelphia. The armada reached Philadelphia in July and proceeded to New York. Failing to engage Clinton there, it sailed to Newport, Rhode Island, where its commander, Jean Baptiste Charles Henri Hector, comte d'Estaing, confronted a larger than expected British garrison. A severe storm blew up before a battle could be pitched, and d'Estaing sailed to Boston for refitting and later to the West Indies to harass the British in the Caribbean.

The closing months of 1778 were uneventful, as were the fall and winter activities at Middlebrook, where Washington caught up on his correspondence. In October, in a letter to Gouverneur Morris, a close friend and a delegate to the Continental Congress, he expressed concern about the outcome of the war, particularly the rising costs of maintaining an army in the field. "What Officer can bear the weight of prices, that every necessary Article is now got to? A Rat, in the shape of a Horse, is not to be bought at this time for less than £200; a Saddle under thirty or Forty; Boots twenty, and Shoes and other articles in like proportion." The real question, he said, was not whether Britain could continue the war, but "whose Finances (theirs or ours) is most likely to fail."

In a letter of November 18 to Virginian Benjamin Harrison, father of future president William Henry Harrison and a signer of the Declaration of Independence, he questioned the quality of the delegates sitting in Congress and urged the states "not only choose, but absolutely compel their ablest Men to attend." He also chided the civilian citizenry for taking the war and its economic implications too lightly. He suggested that while the army was suffering from restrictions placed upon it by the financial crisis and some officers were "sinking by sure degrees into beggary and want," people on the home front were more interested in attending "an assembly, a concert, a Dinner, or Supper (that will cost three or four hundred pounds)."

To Thomas Nelson, also a signer of the Declaration and the commander of Virginia militia, he confided in March 1779 that at no other time were "cool and dispassionate reasoning, strict attention and application, great integrity, and . . . wisdom" more essential. "Our affairs . . . are now come to a crisis," he said, "and require no small degree of political skill, to steer clear of those shelves and Rock which . . . may wreck our hopes, and throw us upon some inhospitable shore."

In late May 1779 General Clinton sent a six-thousand-man expedition up the Hudson River from New York City with orders to clear the river of American occupation. Two patriot forts, Stony Point and Verplanck's Point, were stormed and captured, but only briefly. Six weeks later, Washington dispatched General Anthony Wayne, a former commandant at Fort Ticonderoga who was instrumental in salvaging the battle at Monmouth for the Americans, to retake the forts. On July 15, Wayne, with 1,300 troops, attacked Stony Point and reoccupied it later in the day, thus crushing British ambitions for control of the Hudson.

For the 1779–80 winter encampment, Washington again selected Morristown, New Jersey. Enduring weather more severe than the winter at Valley Forge, the army was again subjected to privation and hunger. "Many a good lad [had] nothing to cover him from his hips to his toes, save his blanket," wrote one officer. In mid-December, in a letter to the governors of New York, New Jersey, Delaware, Maryland, and Pennsylvania, in which he practically begged for assistance, Washington wrote:

> The situation of the Army with respect to supplies is beyond description alarming. . . . Our Magazines are absolutely empty every where and our commissaries entirely destitute of Money or Credit to replenish them. . . . Unless some extraordinary and immediate exertions be made by the States, from which we draw our supplies, there is every appearance that the Army will infallibly disband in a fortnight."

Terrible snowstorms plagued the camp all winter, and many men survived by sharing forage with their animals.

Five months of hunger, freezing cold, and lack of pay were more than some of the army could tolerate. On May 25, 1780, two regiments of the Connecticut line mutinied and threatened to return to their homes. Quick action by the officers defused the situation, but Washington despaired that, unless sufficient relief came soon, similar incidents would occur.

Following the battle at Monmouth, General Clinton had turned his attention toward the southern states, hoping that the sizable base of Tory support in the region and the minimal American military presence there would offer his redcoats opportunities to make serious inroads that had been impossible elsewhere. Savannah, Georgia, had already been captured by the British in late 1778, and the town's new defenders had fought off a Franco-American attempt to reoccupy it one year later. During the spring of 1780, from his headquarters in New York City, Clinton had accompanied most of the British fleet and several thousand troops to Charleston, South Carolina, the other great seaport in the South. There, his strategy proved valid, and on May 12, the city surrendered with more than five thousand Americans captured.

Within days after learning of Charleston's fall, Washington confided to Joseph Jones, a congressional delegate:

> Certain I am, that unless Congress speaks in a more decisive tone; unless they are vested with powers by the several States, competent to the great purposes of war, or assume them as matter of right; and they, and the States respectively, act with more energy than they hitherto have done, that our cause is lost. . . . I see one head gradually changing into thirteen. I see one Army branching into thirteen; and instead of its looking up to Congress, as the supreme controuling power of the United States, are considering themselves as dependent on their respective States. In a word, I see the powers of Congress declining too fast for the consequence and respect which is due to them as the Great representative Body of America, and am fearful of the consequences.

"A Reduction of
the British Army . . .
Is Most Happily Effected"

Nothing in Washington's career—his adventures in the wilderness as a surveyor, his years of deliberations in the Virginia House of Burgesses, his success as an affluent plantation owner, or his role as commander in chief of the Continental Army—could have prepared him for the events of September 25, 1780.

He was returning to headquarters in New Jersey after a trip to Hartford, Connecticut, where he and the French general Jean-Baptiste-Donatien de Vimeur, comte de Rochambeau, had conferred earlier in the month about the assignment of a newly arrived five-thousand-man French army off the coast of Rhode Island. He knew that the British had never lost hope of occupying the Hudson River valley, thereby separating New England from the rest of the country. An American position in the region that General Clinton especially coveted was the bastion of West Point, situated less than fifty miles up the Hudson from New

York City. Aware of its strategic value and the critical role it played in the protection of the river valley, Washington announced that, upon his return to headquarters from Hartford, he would inspect West Point.

The Point's commander, General Benedict Arnold, was among Washington's oldest and most faithful friends and the officer entrusted with the important missions to Fort Ticonderoga and Quebec earlier in the war. Following the redcoats' evacuation of Philadelphia, Arnold had assumed command of the patriot army stationed there and married a young Tory woman who, before they met, had been romantically involved with the British adjutant general, Major John André.

At about noon on September 25, when Washington arrived at Arnold's West Point quarters, he was told that his friend had recently departed downriver, but that he would be returning soon. Later that evening at dinner, he found Mrs. Arnold at home, but servants announced that she was indisposed. A few minutes before the meal, a packet of letters was delivered to him and, as he opened and read them one by one, his face reddened and his hands trembled. When General Lafayette, who was traveling with him, entered the room, Washington exclaimed, "Arnold has betrayed us! Whom can we trust now?"

The incriminating letters, revealing that Arnold was plotting to surrender the West Point garrison to the British, were discovered in the possession of a man calling himself John Anderson, but who later was identified as Major André. Earlier, André had proceeded to West Point to confer with Arnold and to survey plans of the fortification and other critical information prior to its turnover. Dressed as a civilian and therefore tried as a spy, he was hanged soon after his capture. Arnold was never apprehended by the Americans. For his treasonous act, he was awarded £6,315, a small pension for his wife and children, and a brigadier's commission in the British army.

Arnold's treason affected Washington significantly, and he felt personally betrayed by this friend of so many years. While the British made political hay out of the issue, hoping that Arnold's initiative would induce other high-ranking American army and government officials to defect, the commander in chief urged his countrymen to refrain from vigilantism, lest "by sowing jealousies, and . . . swallow[ing] the bait, no character will be safe. There will be nothing but mutual distrust." He said all Americans should be thankful that the plot was discovered before damage could be done.

Following Charleston's fall to the British in May 1780, Clinton returned to New York City, leaving General Charles Cornwallis in command of the southern army.

Three months later, at Camden, South Carolina, General Horatio Gates suffered a monumental defeat by the redcoats, causing him to retreat in such haste that his troops were scattered for miles across the countryside.

In early October, at Kings Mountain, also in South Carolina, two American armies—one patriot, the other loyalist—faced each other. In a vicious sixty-five-minute battle, the patriots emerged victorious after killing, wounding, or capturing practically the entire Tory force. The conflict proved to be the turning point of the war in the South, leaving thousands of American loyalists aghast at the decisive defeat and delaying Cornwallis's proposed invasion of North Carolina.

In December, still fretting over Gates's ignominious defeat and retreat at Camden, Washington replaced the discredited veteran with General Nathanael Greene, a no-nonsense former Rhode Island blacksmith and ironmonger. Washington retired his northern army for the winter and established headquarters near West Point, but had barely settled in when he learned from the Morristown encampment that on January 1, 1781, several privates and noncommissioned officers of the Pennsylvania line had mutinied, killing and wounding a few of their officers. Their complaints centered on the old problems of no pay, poor food, and terms of enlistment. Marching on Philadelphia, they placed their grievances before state officials and demanded settlement, part of which was the discharge of nearly 2,500 soldiers.

The mutineers' demands were met, a decision that inspired additional uprisings, one of which occurred three weeks later among New Jersey troops. This time, Washington took control of the situation, ordering a detachment of his army to round up the culprits and instructing the troops' commander to "grant no terms while they are with Arms in their hands in a state of resistance. . . . If you succeed in compelling the revolted Troops to a surrender you will instantly execute a few of the most active and incendiary leaders."

In mid-January, the general in chief was elated to learn that General Daniel Morgan, a French and Indian War veteran and a cousin of Daniel Boone, soundly defeated the British at Cowpens, South Carolina, as his force captured eight hundred redcoats. Two months later, Greene's command annihilated about five hundred of Cornwallis's finest troopers at Guilford Court-house, North Carolina, in a heated action described by Cornwallis as a British victory. To this spurious claim, Greene replied, "I pray God the enemy wins many more such triumphs." Despite another trouncing by Greene at Eutaw Springs, South Carolina, on September 8, British forces remained resilient.

In April, Washington learned from his cousin, Lund Washington, the caretaker at Mount Vernon, that a British ship had recently anchored in the Potomac River, directly in front of the manor house and threatened it and its residents. Hoping to save the estate, Lund had gone out to the ship with "refreshments," a decision that angered the commander in chief. "It would have been a less painful circumstance to me, to have heard, that in consequence of your non-compliance with their request, they had burnt my House, and laid the Plantation in ruins," he wrote. "You ought to have considered yourself as my representative, and should have reflected on the bad example of communicating with the enemy, and making a voluntary offer of refreshments to them with a view to prevent a conflagration."

In August, the movements of Washington's and Rochambeau's troops in the area convinced Clinton in New York City that an attack there was imminent. Late in the month, however, Washington learned that the French fleet under the command of Admiral François-Joseph-Paul, comte de Grasse, was headed for the Chesapeake Bay, prompting him to combine the American and French armies and march toward Yorktown, Virginia, where Lafayette held Cornwallis's 8,500-man force at bay. The Franco-American army passed through Philadelphia, permitting Washington to report in person to Congress. By September 10, he had reached Mount Vernon. It was his first visit to the plantation in six years, and he cherished the time he spent with Martha and the four children of his stepson, Jack. And, to the commander's great surprise, Jack announced that he was going to join Washington as a civilian aide. After this brief sojourn with his family, the general was ready to confront the British once more. Just prior to setting out for Yorktown, he dispatched a note to Lafayette: "I hope you will keep Lord Cornwallis safe, without Provisions or Forage until we arrive."

Yorktown, a small, sleepy tobacco town, was situated twelve miles from Williamsburg, on a peninsula formed by the James and York Rivers. Following his romp across North and South Carolina, Cornwallis had fallen back on the village to await a British fleet bringing additional manpower and equipment for his southern campaigns. When the armada failed to appear and de Grasse's forces anchored offshore and blockaded the town instead, he watched in horror as the Franco-American forces slowly surrounded his outnumbered army.

The siege on Yorktown began on September 30 and continued for nearly three weeks. On the battle's first day, Washington, concerned that large numbers of the enemy might escape across the York River to nearby Gloucester, ordered his staff to "give immediate Notice to the Inhabitants to remove from their [the British soldiers'] probable Route all the Cattle and Horses that can be of use to them; and at the same time give every impediment to their march that you possibly can, that I may have time to throw my Army in their Front." For days, de Grasse's big guns, transported to Yorktown from the French army head-quarters at Newport, pounded the British outer defenses, and when that perimeter caved in and its defenders retreated to the second tier of earthworks, the French cannoneers began their destruction all over again. Slowly the net drew tighter. On the seventeenth day, Cornwallis requested a twenty-four-hour truce "to settle terms of the surrender." On October 19, to drum and fife music playing "The World Turned Upside Down," a popular song of the times, the once-proud British Army marched without flags or guidons between long lines of French and American soldiers and laid down their arms. Cornwallis notified Washington that he was too ill to attend the ceremonies and sent an adjutant, General Charles O'Hara, to symbolically surrender his sword to the American commander. Adhering to strict military protocol, Washington assigned one of his staff, General Benjamin Lincoln, who had experienced the agony of Charleston's fall to the British, to officially accept the surrender. On the same day, he notified Congress that "A Reduction of the British Army under the Command of Lord Cornwallis is most happily effected." He estimated that nearly six thousand redcoats, "exclusive of Seamen and others," had been taken prisoner. The actual figures were closer to 7,200 men captured, as well as 244 cannons and untold thousands of small arms.

Washington, overjoyed by the joint American-French victory at Yorktown, was equally delighted a week later when he learned that a British fleet carrying General Clinton's relief corps of seven thousand redcoats had arrived near the mouth of the York River, only to turn around and head back to New York upon learning of Cornwallis's defeat.

Washington knew that the significance of what the combined American and French armies, assisted by the French navy, had accomplished could not be overstated. The allied victory shocked Parliament and the British army as their dreams of a unified South, up in arms against the Continental Army and its patriot sympathizers, vanished like cannon smoke over the deserted redoubts at Yorktown. But Washington also realized that Clinton still maintained a sizable army in New York and that Admiral de Grasse had refused to proceed northward with his fleet to attack the British. The commander insisted that neither the American army nor Congress allow the recent victory to diminish the resolve to continue the war and use whatever means necessary to expel the British forever. Echoing these sentiments, he described Yorktown as "an interesting event that may be productive of much good if properly improved, but if it should be the means of relaxation and sink us into supineness and [false] security, it had better not have happened."

BENEDICT ARNOLD

Although Benedict Arnold served the American army for many years and was responsible for several important victories over the British during the Revolution, his name will forever be linked with his attempted surrender of West Point to enemy forces in September 1780. Historians have tried for over two hundred years to explain why this brilliant and much-decorated soldier sold out his country and defected; the majority of them agree that debt and failure to receive a promotion were the primary factors.

He was born to a prominent family in Norwich, Connecticut, in January 1741, his great-grandfather a one-time colonial governor of Rhode Island. Arnold became a druggist and successful merchant, often financing trading trips to the West Indies and Canada. Prior to the Revolutionary War, he had twice served in the colonial militia, deserting both times. As the war with Great Britain progressed, he once again joined the militia as a captain and accompanied his men to Massachusetts, where they participated in the skirmishes at Concord and Lexington. Rapidly attaining the rank of colonel, he assisted Ethan Allen and his Green Mountain Boys in the capture of Fort Ticonderoga in May 1775.

Later in the same year, Arnold was severely wounded when he and his forces unsuccessfully tried to capture Quebec. Following his recuperation, he was promoted to brigadier general and received command of a gunboat fleet patrolling Lake Champlain, there displaying great skill against the British vessels in the region. In February 1777, while he was protecting a militia depot in Connecticut, two horses were shot from beneath him; for his skill and bravery he was promoted to major general and received the thanks of Congress.

He was instrumental in General Horatio Gates's stunning victory at Saratoga during the fall of 1777, but received little credit. The lack of recognition and the earlier promotion over him of five junior officers, combined with the great debt acquired following his assignment to Philadelphia as commandant, may have set the stage for his later defection.

After his flight from West Point, Arnold commanded the Crown's forces in Virginia, where he skirmished with elements of the Continental Army on various occasions. After the war, he and his family moved to England, where they were initially held in high regard, even commanding an audience with King George III. In time, however, the fickle British public lost all interest in him and treated him indifferently. He died in London on June 14, 1801, largely forgotten, but a man who, under different circumstances, might have been one of America's leading heroes of the Revolution.

"With a Heart Full of . . . Gratitude,
I Now Take Leave of You"

Washington's jubilation over the Franco-American victory at Yorktown was short-lived. Following the battle, he maintained quarters locally while he conferred with his staff, organized the troops, made arrangements for the care of British prisoners and wounded, and disposed of the captured war matériel. He ordered most of the army back to headquarters in New York, while dispatching a smaller contingent to South Carolina to strengthen General Nathanael Greene's command there.

In early November 1781, Jack Custis, who had served as his stepfather's civilian aide at Yorktown, died following a brief illness, most likely typhus, or "camp fever." The body was transported to a neighboring plantation and from there Washington wrote to his personal secretary, John Trumbull, Jr., "I came here in time to see Mr. Custis breathe his last. . . . The deep and solemn distress of the Mother, and affliction of the Wife of this amiable young Man, requires every comfort in my power to afford them." The general took personal charge of arranging for Custis's final rites and, following a proper mourning period, returned to planning a complete victory over the British and attaining independence for the struggling United States.

While observing the recent action at Yorktown, he had been impressed by the performance of the French fleet and prophesied that the combatant commanding the most successful navy would win the war. He shared his strong feelings in a letter written in mid-November to General Lafayette: "No Land force can act decisively, unless it is accompanied by a Maritime superiority; nor can more than negative advantages be expected without it. . . . A constant naval superiority would terminate the War speedily; without it, I do not know that it will ever be terminated honourably."

Accompanied by a still grieving Martha, Washington departed Mount Vernon on November 20, bound for Philadelphia, where he would confer with the country's civilian leaders over the war's future. During their journey, the couple visited Annapolis and other communities where he was given a hero's welcome. In the capital, he assigned his northern army to winter camp at Newburgh, New York, and began the tedious work of lobbying Congress for additional funds to support his troops and reward those veterans who had recently mustered out of the service.

Although the United States was already five years old, Washington found Congress still severely fragmented, each state's representatives seeming more interested in affairs at home than in the nation's overall welfare. In 1777, in an attempt to meld the country into a whole and to eliminate regional differences and petty squabbles, the body had approved a far-reaching accord, the Articles of Confederation. Upon its ratification by the states in March 1781, the document became law, but eight months later, it had achieved little progress toward unification.

While in the capital, Washington learned that Congress had recently requested eight million dollars from the individual states to help finance the war for the year 1782. On January 22, in letters to the governors, he reiterated the necessity for the appropriations, reminding them of "the ferment into which the whole Army was thrown twelve Months ago, for the want of pay and a regular supply of Clothing and Provisions." Less than two months later, anticipating another year of campaigning with the British, he wrote, "Never, since the commencement of the present revolution, has there been, in my judgment, a period when more vigorous measures were more consonant with sound policy than the present." Yet, as warm weather and an uncertain future for the army approached, Congress seemed little interested in satisfying Washington's requests for assistance.

While he petitioned Congress and the governors of the thirteen states for needed funds to finance what he believed to be a protracted war, rumors arrived in Philadelphia from Europe that Great Britain would soon sue for peace. Eventually it was learned that in early March 1782 Parliament had in fact authorized the British government to seek peace with the United States and that the prime minister, Lord North, had been replaced by Charles Watson-Wentworth, Lord Rockingham, known for his sympathy for American independence.

Despite such favorable signs, Washington refused to believe that Britain was serious about ending the war and, well into May, was still making detailed strategies for battles that would never be fought. The peace talks, he wrote, were merely propaganda tools designed "to quiet the Minds of our own people." He also observed of the British, "Finding themselves hard pushed in other quarters, they want to amuse us in America, whilst they attend to other parts of their Empire; which being secured, they will have time and means to revert to this continent again, with hopes of success." But England's call for peace was sincere, and in April, Benjamin Franklin, who had assisted in negotiating France's entry into the conflict, began diplomatic talks with British and French representatives in Paris. On July 11, the redcoats evacuated Charleston and Savannah, and in November preliminary Articles of Peace were signed.

Meanwhile, Washington tried to keep his inactive troops busy at Newburgh. With no battles to fight, the summer provided time for extra training, maintenance of equipment, and weapons practice, along with less serious activities for the men, worn out from combat, hunger, and disease. The commander displayed a personal interest in his men and participated in the minutest detail of their affairs, writing in his General Orders of June 8, 1782, "The Officers commanding the Light Infantry should impress upon the men the necessity of taking deliberate Aim whenever they fire and see that they do it when it is in their power." Although the troops appreciated the need for extra training, their most pressing problem for the moment, one that critically affected them and their families, was simply getting paid for their months and years of service as protectors of the country.

Most of Washington's troops, from the lowest private to highest-ranking general, were disturbed by the pay issue, as well as their poor rations, filthy living conditions, and slow or nonexistent promotions. They had suffered most during the long and grueling conflict, yet when their years of selfless and dedicated service were over, they had little or nothing to show for their efforts. Adding to the troubles was the decision to keep the entire Continental Army in uniform until peace could be officially declared, an event that did not occur for nearly two years after the actual fighting had ceased.

In May 1782, Washington received correspondence from Colonel Lewis Nicola, an Irishman respected and well liked by both his men and his commander in chief. The letter made Washington shudder. Nicola revealed that he had detected an attitude among army troops that the new, hard-won American government should be set up as a monarchy and that Washington should be installed as its first king.

The general was flabbergasted. In a terse reply to Nicola, he declared, "With a mixture of great surprise and astonishment, I have read with attention the Sentiments you have submitted to my perusal. . . . Be assured Sir, no occurrence in the course of the War, has given me more painful sensations than your information of there being such ideas existing in the Army as you have expressed, and I must view with abhorrence, and reprehend with severity." The notion of installing Washington as king of America was short-lived and literally died with his angry response to Nicola. "If you have any regard for your Country, concern for yourself or posterity, or respect for me . . . banish these thoughts from your Mind, and never communicate, as from yourself, or any one else, a sentiment of the like Nature," he cautioned.

Meantime, the army's problems remained unresolved, and the weary soldiers of the Continental Army hardened their attitude toward Congress and its leaders. The following year, at headquarters in Newburgh, Washington faced another crisis, known as the Newburgh Conspiracy, when he learned that a number of officers and enlisted men planned to mutiny over the issues that had plagued them for so long. In a speech to his men on March 15, 1783, Washington pleaded with them to be patient and to give the infant government time to get on its feet so that it could conform to their wishes. During the address, a weary and worn Washington reached in his pocket for his newly acquired spectacles and remarked, "I have grown not only gray, but almost blind in my country's service." The tender comments completely defused the situation and support for the mutiny fizzled.

Time passed slowly while Washington and the rest of the army awaited news that peace terms had been consummated. When reports finally arrived in April 1783, confirming the provisional accords reached the previous November, the commander issued General Orders declaring "the Cessation of Hostilities between the United States of America and the King of Great Britain" to take effect at noon on April 19. He thanked all of his fellow soldiers, particularly "those gallant and persevering men who had resolved to defend the rights of their invaded country so long as the war should continue—For these are the men who ought to be considered as the [pride] . . . of the American Army; And, who crowned with well earned laurels, may soon withdraw from the field of Glory, to the more tranquil walks of civil life."

Congress ordered Washington to dismiss as many troops as he could, although the money to pay them was nonexistent. Some soldiers returned home with nothing to show for their years of service; others, with the thanks of the government, received only the rifle or musket they had carried with them throughout the conflict. For Washington, it was a sad time. After all, it was he who had promised only one month earlier, during the dangerous days of the Newburgh Conspiracy, that Congress would make good on all of its promises if the troops would just support the army for a while longer.

The official peace treaty formally ending the war was signed in Paris on September 3, 1783. By its terms, the United States acquired all of the land east of the Mississippi River except for the extreme northwestern portion (today's states of Wisconsin, Illinois, Michigan, and part of Indiana) and Spanish Florida. In late November, British troops evacuated New York City, the last Crown-held territory in the United States, and were replaced by an American army led by General Henry Knox.

On December 4, Washington met with a few of his officers for the last time at Fraunces Tavern in New York City, announcing as he embraced each man, "With a heart full of love and gratitude, I now take leave of you." He added, "I most devoutly wish that your later days may be as prosperous and happy as your former ones have been glorious and honorable." Leaving New York immediately afterward, he was bestowed with honors in practically every town through which he passed. In Annapolis, Maryland, where Congress was holding session, he officially resigned "with satisfaction the appointment I accepted with diffidence; a diffidence in my abilities to accomplish so arduous a task, which however was superseded by a confidence in the rectitude of our cause, the support of the Supreme power of the Union, and the patronage of Heaven."

At last the war was over and the victorious commander was returning to his beloved Martha and their cherished Mount Vernon. He was a civilian again, and thoughts of spring planting, playing with Jack's children, and all of the many pleasures he had missed for the past eight years flooded his mind as he pressed his horse forward from Annapolis. As he reached his plantation, it occurred to him that it was Christmas Eve. What better gift could he have desired than the one he was about to receive?

"I Am at Length Become a Private Citizen . . . on the Banks of the Patowmac"

lthough it had been nearly a decade since he personally had managed the estate, Washington assumed his old responsibilities with ambition and vigor. His cousin, Lund Washington, had performed well his duties as caretaker during the general's prolonged absence, yet the restored private citizen was anxious to once again give his beloved homeplace the personal touches that only he could provide.

In 1774 he had added a wing to the south end of Mount Vernon, making the building temporarily asymmetrical until an equalizing north wing could be built, construction of which began in 1776. Now, although the addition's exterior was complete, the inside still needed work, and Washington contracted with local workmen to hang the windows and doors, paint walls, and "finish the other parts." When completed, the western façade of the building attained its present-day look except for the cupola and weathervane, which were installed in 1787.

Domestic chores and farm duties aside, Washington's mind was still troubled by the uncertain future faced by the infant United States now that the war was over and independence had been won. Less than three weeks after his return home, he wrote to Virginia's governor Benjamin Harrison about the nagging concern he had over the rights and responsibilities of states versus those of the federal government, as well as the volatile situation that could occur if these responsibilities were not clearly defined and enforced:

> The disinclination of the individual States to yield competent powers to Congress for the Federal Government, their unreasonable jealousy of that body & of one another & the disposition which seems to pervade each, of being all-wise and all-powerful within itself, will, if there is not a change in the system be our downfal as a Nation.

He also was fearful that Great Britain and other European powers might detect the growing differences in political philosophy throughout America and recognize them as weaknesses, perhaps using the occasion for intervention. "I have many [fears], & powerful ones indeed which predict the worst consequences from a half-starved, limping Government, that appears to be always moving upon crutches, & tottering at every step," he wrote.

Despite his continued interest in national affairs, he was retired and recognized that he would have little involvement with whatever problems might occur during the charting of the new nation. He would relax at home and live the tranquil life he loved. "I am at length become a private citizen of America, on the banks of the Patowmac," he wrote to his friend the Marquis de Chastellux, a former general in the French army who had seen duty in the United States. From "under my own Vine & my own Fig tree—free from the bustle of a camp & the intrigues of a Court, I shall view the busy world . . . with that serenity of mind, which the Soldier in his pursuit of glory, & the Statesman of fame, have not time to enjoy."

Mount Vernon fairly seethed with activity. Although Washington and Martha remained childless, the home to which he returned after the war was still blessed with the laughter of the late Jack's son, George Washington Parke Custis (called "Little Washington"), and daughter, Eleanor Parke Custis (called "Nelly"). Streams of relatives, close friends, and even remote acquaintances visited often and stayed for long periods, sometimes trying George's and Martha's patience and hospitality. More than two hundred field slaves, along with scores of overseers, craftsmen, and house servants, required shelter, food, and clothing. An assemblage of separate buildings in which slaves, spinners, blacksmiths, shoemakers, tailors, carpenters, and others lived and worked were clustered about the main house and in constant need of repair. Livestock by the hundreds roamed the vast acreage of the estate, now expanded to include five dependent, yet separately operated, farms that stretched for ten miles along the Potomac River and as much as four miles inland.

Washington soon fell into his prewar daily routine. Up at dawn, he bathed, shaved, had his hair brushed by his servant,

Will, and ate breakfast, usually consisting of "three small Indian hoecakes (buttered) and as many dishes of tea (without cream)." He then spent the remainder of each day riding across the various farms, checking on the slaves' welfare, conferring with overseers, sharing information about some agricultural scheme he had recently discovered, and keeping a detailed journal of all his activities. He returned home for dinner, always served at 2 P.M., to a table which, "whether there be company or not, [was] always prepared by its elegance and exuberance for their reception," a visitor said. He usually ate lightly, finishing off his meal with a glass of Madeira. Following more field supervision, he appeared once again in the late afternoon to be served "one small glass of punch, a draught of beer, and two dishes of tea." Since visitors were so frequent at Mount Vernon, supper was always a glorious affair, although Washington seldom appeared, but rather retired at around 9 P.M.

His curiosity and interest in agriculture and animal husbandry never waned. Once he announced to bewildered farm employees that a bushel of timothy contained 13,411,000 individual grains. On another occasion he became keenly interested in mules, an animal difficult to procure in the United States at the time. Since mules are the offspring of a male ass and a female horse, they are themselves sterile. Learning through diplomatic channels of Washington's desire to improve the bloodline of American mules, the king of Spain, anxious to impress the man whom most Spaniards looked upon as the liberator of America, gifted him with a pair of his prize jackasses. The animals were shipped across the Atlantic, one dying in transit, the other arriving in

Boston. Washington arranged for it to be transported to Mount Vernon, but to his disappointment, the animal, given the name Royal Gift, showed little interest in any of the mares that were placed in his paddock. Although his early experiments with mule production were less than what Washington had hoped for, the blood of Royal Gift still flows in most championship mules in America today.

Soon after his return to Mount Vernon from the war, Washington journeyed across the Allegheny Mountains to check on his land holdings and was surprised by the degree of growth that had occurred in the once uninhabited region. A new town called Pittsburgh sat on the site of Fort Duquesne, which he had assisted General John Forbes in occupying near the end of the French and Indian War. And scattered throughout the wilderness of the upper Ohio River valley were the log homes of the pioneers who had cleared the land, brought in their families, and started a new life on the edge of the frontier. Already, some of these farmers faced difficulty disposing of their produce downriver in New Orleans, since the Spanish, who still controlled the lower Mississippi valley, refused Americans access to the city. As Washington thought about the hardships and restrictions faced by the Ohio River farmers—fully aware that the population, along with the problems, would only increase as time passed—he resurrected an idea that he thought might hold the key to the region's future.

Upon returning home from his travels, he began exploring the scheme that had absorbed him during the previous few months:

if the headwaters of the eastward-flowing rivers of tidewater Virginia could be linked through a series of canals with the westward-flowing streams on the far side of the Alleghenies, farmers and merchants in the backcountry would be linked with the markets of the East, thereby ending their dependence upon the Ohio-Mississippi River system for the transportation of their produce. The idea was not new. As early as 1765, the Virginia General Assembly had discussed it, but to no avail. Even Washington himself, just before the Revolution, had attempted to interest private subscribers in funding a 150-mile-long watercourse connecting Will's Creek, Pennsylvania, with the Atlantic. Now, however, with the backcountry population growing with every passing month, the need for such facilities was more important than ever before. What time would be more ideal to implement a canal system than the present?

On October 10, 1784, he wrote to Governor Benjamin Harrison, "It has been long my decided opinion that the shortest, easiest, and least expensive communication with the invaluable and extensive Country back of us, would be by one, or both of the rivers of this State [the James and the Potomac] which have their sources in the Apalachian mountains." Some months later, the Patowmack Company was organized, charged with improving navigation on the Potomac River, with Washington elected its president. Since Virginia and Maryland shared the river as a common boundary, he held a conference at Mount Vernon later in 1785 to head off any problems that might arise between the two jurisdictions. A second meeting was held the following year in Annapolis and involved the participation by several additional states. Finally a third assembly, convened in Philadelphia in 1787, evolved into the Constitutional Convention.

Only minimal progress was made on Washington's navigation proposals during his lifetime; in fact, groundbreaking for the facility that grew out of his Potomac River concept—the Chesapeake and Ohio Canal—was delayed until 1828. The waterway finally reached Cumberland, Maryland, in 1850.

GEORGE WASHINGTON ON SLAVERY

From the time Washington's great-grandfather, John, first set foot on Virginia soil in 1656, the Washington family owned slaves, a tradition that was to continue throughout George's lifetime.

Slavery in the American colonies had its beginning in 1619, when a Dutch pirate ship docked at the twelve-year-old village of Jamestown in Virginia. On board the galleon were many African slaves, twenty of whom were put ashore in exchange for supplies. Although at the time they were simply indentured servants and not slaves in the strictest sense, they were immediately assigned to the fields, where they labored side by side with white workers.

In the ensuing years, the number of Africans brought to America gradually increased. By 1626, slaves had been introduced in New Amsterdam, in Connecticut in 1629, in

Maryland in 1634, and in Massachusetts in 1638. The colonists, pleased with the large amounts of available free labor, began to look on the disenfranchised blacks as true chattels, to be bought and sold like any other property. In 1641 Massachusetts became the first colony to officially recognize slavery as a legal institution, followed by Virginia some twenty years later.

Although some slaveholders were kind and humane—and all existing evidence places Washington in this category—others looked upon their human property as they did their livestock or real estate. The African men, women, and even the children were often abused, whipped, starved, and sometimes murdered. They were kept ignorant, forbidden to learn to read or obtain an education. Sometimes families were separated when one parent, or perhaps both, was placed on the auction block, leaving the children behind.

Washington adamantly refused to sell his slaves, which explains why they were so populous at Mount Vernon. Additional insight into his feelings on the subject is revealed in an April 1786 letter to a friend.

> I can only say that there is not a man living who wishes more sincerely than I do, to see a plan adopted for the abolition of it [slavery]. . . . But when slaves who are happy and contented with their present

masters, are tampered with and seduced to leave them; when masters are taken unawares by these practices; when a conduct of this sort begets discontent on one side and resentment on the other, and when it happens to fall on a man, whose purse will not measure with that of the Society, and he looses his property for want of means to defend it; it is oppression in the latter case, and not humanity in any; because it introduces more evils than it can cure.

In his last will and testament Washington specified that all of his slaves be freed.

"If Nothing Had Been Agreed On . . . Anarchy Would Soon Have Ensued"

Although Washington's cousin Lund had adequately overseen the day-to-day operations of Mount Vernon during the general's absence in the war, the records, inventories, and financial papers of the plantation had been sadly neglected. In time, Washington hired a new secretary, Tobias Lear, to assemble, sort, and prioritize the material. A native of New Hampshire, Lear was initially unimpressed and somewhat intimidated by the master of Mount Vernon, but in later years, after the two men had become close friends, Lear described his employer as "more than a man," one who displayed "honesty, uprightness, and candor in all of his private transactions." As Lear began the task of organizing Washington's documents, he discovered that his employer had lost over ten thousand pounds sterling during the war, much of the sum spent outfitting his men with food and supplies. The general had graciously refused a salary when he assumed the role of commander in chief of the Continental Army, requesting that he be reimbursed only for expenses. Now, Lear discovered, the cash-poor Congress had paid many of their debts to Washington in certificates of indebtedness. These, in time of need, the commander had been forced to sell at great discounts while he continued the lavish and costly parties that he and Martha threw for family and friends. Even so, he adamantly refused to accept late remuneration for his years in the army.

Other, less personal issues plagued him as well. Wresting independence from England had not solved the problems of the infant United States. Since the peace, the shaky government had functioned under the loosely written Articles of Confederation. The document was approved by Congress in 1777, when it became painfully obvious that thirteen widely separated colonies, each with its own agenda, could not efficiently wage an organized war against so powerful an enemy as Great Britain. When they were finally ratified in March 1781, it was hoped that the articles would unify the individual states for the single purpose of resolving the complex issues of nationhood.

Despite the good intentions of the Articles' framers, the guidelines proved futile in bringing the individual states into a cohesive unit. As one pundit commented, "The United States were free, but they certainly were not 'united.'" Money was practically nonexistent since the Articles provided no mechanism for defining and collecting taxes or other income-producing measures. That the nation was suffering financially could not be denied; in fact, the interest on the national debt could not even be paid. To add to these problems, Congress invariably had difficulty assembling the quorum of delegates required to legally convene. Differences between the states, as evidenced by the vast numbers of local laws, religious preferences, tariff restrictions, and long-range goals, made centralized control virtually impossible.

Washington remained concerned about the rights and obligations of the individual states versus those of the federal government. His opinions had not changed since July 1783, when he had written from his camp at Newburgh, New York:

> I think it may properly be asked for what purpose do we farcically pretend to be United? Why do Congress spend Months together in deliberating upon, debating, and digesting plans, which are made as palatable, and as wholesome to the Constitution of this Country as the nature of things will admit of, when some States will pay no attention to them, and others regard them but partially; by which means all those evils which proceed from delay, are felt by the whole; while the compliant States are not only suffering by these neglects, but in many instances are injured most capitally by their own exertions; which are wasted for want of the United effort.

By 1786 the nation's leaders conceded that the Articles of Confederation, without serious reform and rewriting, were doomed to failure, and they hoped to consider many of the outstanding issues at the Annapolis convention, held in September. Ostensibly the meeting's purpose was to continue the canal and navigational debates begun the previous year at Mount Vernon, but other important matters involving the states were placed on the docket as well. When only five states sent delegates to the assembly, however, it was adjourned and another meeting was set for the following May in Philadelphia, specifically to bring the Articles of Confederation into compliance with "the exigencies of the Union."

Washington did not attend the Annapolis convention and was disappointed to learn of its premature collapse. At about the same time that the news of its failure reached him, he received a message telling of a civil disturbance in Massachusetts, reinforcing his conviction that a strong, centralized government should take precedence over individual states' authority. Daniel Shays, a former Revolutionary captain, had led a group of angry insurgents, protesting over the seizure of private property among New Englanders to satisfy their outstanding debts and taxes; in Springfield they demonstrated before the state supreme court. The mob eventually disbanded, but not before it became apparent that Massachusetts authorities were ill-prepared to deal with a problem that transcended state borders.

As the Philadelphia convention neared, Washington debated whether or not he should even attend. He had announced his retirement years ago and wondered if his reentry into public affairs would be considered by his friends and admirers as vacillation. Yet he was intently interested in the meeting's outcome and sensed that dynamic changes would evolve from it. He observed to a friend, "How far the revision of the federal system, and giving more adequate powers to Congress may be productive of an efficient government, I will not under my present view of the matter, presume to decide. That many inconveniences result from the present form, none can deny."

Days before he would have to depart Mount Vernon if he

did in fact decide to attend the assembly, he took to his bed, seriously ill, further complicating his predicament. "Indeed my health is become very precarious," he wrote his old Revolutionary War friend Henry Knox in April 1787. "A rheumatic complaint which has followed me more than 6 months is frequently so bad that it is sometimes with difficulty I can raise my hand to my head, or turn myself in bed. . . . This . . . might . . . prevent my attendance."

Despite his illness, and anticipating far-reaching ramifications from the convention, he left Mount Vernon on May 9, arriving in Philadelphia in time for the first session on May 14. It remained to be seen whether the delegates would perform their work to strengthen the country.

Expecting that the convention would be drawn out, Washington accepted the invitation of his friend Robert Morris, a wealthy merchant and signer of the Declaration of Independence, to use his home as temporary quarters while in the city. Delegates from only two states, Virginia and Pennsylvania, were present at the opening session on the fourteenth, and not until eleven days later had sufficient members arrived to constitute a quorum. Washington was unanimously elected president of the meeting.

During the next four months—sometimes for up to seven hours a day, six days a week—delegates grappled with the reorganization of the government: how many legislative houses to recognize, how many branches of government to designate, and whether there should be a single chief executive or three, one each from the north, south, and west. Some members argued for less federal authority, prompting Washington to write, "The Men who oppose a strong & energetic government are, in my opinion, narrow minded politicians, or are under the influence of local views. The apprehension expressed by them that the *people* will not accede to the form proposed is the *ostensible*, not the *real* cause of the opposition—but admitting that the present sentiment is as they prognosticate, the question ought nevertheless to be, is it or is it not, the best form?"

On Monday, September 17, 1787, the new Constitution was finally approved and Washington recorded in his diary, "The business being thus closed, the Members adjourned to the City Tavern, dined together and took a cordial leave of each other." He left Philadelphia the following day for Mount Vernon and, as soon as he arrived home, sent a copy of the document to his friend and fellow Revolutionary Patrick Henry, admitting, "I wish the Constitution which is offered had been more perfect, but I sincerely believe it is the best that could be obtained at this time; and, as a constitutional door is opened for amendment hereafter, the adoption of it under the present circumstances of the Union, is in my opinion desirable."

To become legal, the Constitution required the ratification of nine states and, by May 1788, eight had voted their approval. The Virginia Assembly met on June 25, and Washington rejoiced when he received news that his home state had cast the vote that implemented the new document, making it the official foundation upon which the Republic's principles were subsequently built. All of the governmental functions recognized today were defined in the Constitution: the provision for a legislative branch of government with a bicameral Congress, the establishment of the judicial and executive branches, and the definition of the duties and responsibilities of the president.

March 4, 1789, was set as the date the new Constitution—and thus, the new government—would go into effect. Although Washington did not encourage his name to be placed forward for the nation's presidency, he was the only person ever seriously considered. He was well aware that he was in the forefront for the position, but he would have been perfectly happy if someone else filled the role. In a letter to Alexander Hamilton, his former aide, he wrote in October 1788, "If I should be prevailed upon to accept it [the presidency]; the acceptance would be attended with more diffidence and reluctance than ever I experienced before in my life. It would be, however, with a fixed and sole determination of lending whatever assistance might be in my power to promote the public weal, in hopes that at a convenient and an early period, my services might be dispensed with, and that I might be permitted once more to retire."

The Constitution stipulated that each elector cast two votes; the candidate receiving the majority would become president, and the runner-up, vice president. Sixty-nine electors, representing ten states, had been qualified by February 4, 1789, the date set for ballots to be taken. New York had not yet selected its electors; neither North Carolina nor Rhode Island had ratified the Constitution, making those three states ineligible to participate. The qualified electors assembled in New York City, the temporary capital, and when the results were tallied, Washington was unanimously elected president, receiving all sixty-nine votes. John Adams received thirty-four votes, giving him the vice presidency. Other candidates on the ballot were John Jay and George Clinton of New York, Robert Hanson Harrison of Maryland, John Rutledge of South Carolina, John Hancock of Massachusetts, Samuel Huntington of Connecticut, and John Milton, James Armstrong, Edward Telfair, and Benjamin Lincoln of Georgia, all strong, patriotic individuals who had been active in the Revolution.

The Constitution specified that the votes were to be officially counted in the presence of the Senate and the House of Representatives on March 4, but by that date, only a small number of congressmen had appeared for the session. At Mount Vernon, on the same day, Washington, still awaiting official notification of his election, anguished over the expected expenses of the trip to New York and his residency there while serving as chief executive. He anticipated having minimal future income since he refused compensation for his presidential service, just as he had declined a salary as commander in chief of the Continental Army. For the past two years, Mount Vernon had failed to make a profit and, despite his best efforts to sell off some of his vast land holdings, he was still cash-poor and experiencing a feeling of financial crisis. Concerned that he would leave home in debt, he wrote to Richard Conway, a friend in nearby Alexandria, that he was "inclined to do what I never expected to be driven to, that is, to borrow money on Interest." He requested a loan from Conway in the amount of five hundred pounds sterling in order "to discharge what I owe in Alexandria, etc." He confided in his friend that "to leave the State without doing this, would be exceedingly disagreeable to me." The president-elect was much relieved when Conway graciously consented to his request.

Finally, in early April, a sufficient number of delegates had assembled in New York for a quorum and the votes could be formally counted, making official what everyone already knew. Washington learned of his election on April 14. Two days later, he left the banks of the Potomac to serve his country once again. He recorded in his journal:

About ten o'clock I bade adieu to Mount Vernon, to private life, and to domestic felicity; and, with a mind oppressed with more anxious and painful sensations than I have words to express, set out for New York . . . with the best disposition to render service to my country in obedience to its call, but with less hope of answering its expectations.

"I Entered upon My Administration . . . with the Best Intentions"

In every town Washington visited en route to New York City, he was given a hero's welcome. He tarried at nearby Alexandria, Virginia, long enough to dine with neighbors and old friends and to bid a sad farewell, telling them that "no earthly consideration, short of a conviction of duty" could ever have persuaded him to forsake his retirement and embark "again on the tempestuous and uncertain ocean of public-life." At Trenton, New Jersey, the site of his daring early-morning attack on the Hessian mercenaries' encampment a dozen years earlier, the daughter of famed artist Charles Willson Peale bestowed a crown of laurel leaves upon his head as he passed beneath a triumphal arch, while thirteen young women, decked out in flowing white gowns, serenaded him with the song "Welcome, Mighty Chief, Once More." Finally approaching New York City on April 23, 1789, amid tumultuous cannon fire, he crossed the bay from Elizabeth Town Point, New Jersey, to Manhattan

Island aboard a barge festively decorated with flags and garlands of flowers. He docked at the foot of Wall Street, where he was welcomed by New York governor George Clinton.

For the next six days, Washington toured the city and its environs, always accompanied by a large entourage of officials, curiosity seekers, and well-wishers. On April 30, at noon, from the second-floor balcony of the Federal Building at the intersection of Wall and Broad Streets, the statuesque Virginian, wearing a "suit of Homespun Cloaths . . . of a fine fabric . . . as handsomely finished, as any European superfine cloth," was sworn in as the nation's first president, using a Bible borrowed from St. John's Lodge of the Free and Accepted Masons. During his brief inaugural address, he promised that "no local prejudices or attachments; no separate views, nor party animosities, will misdirect the comprehensive and equal Eye which ought to watch over this great assemblage of communities and interests."

When Martha finally arrived in the capital from Mount Vernon near the end of May, she and her husband defined three kinds of social events that they would host weekly. Men only were invited to the President's House, located at No. 1 Cherry Street, on Tuesdays from three to four o'clock. No invitation was required, but attendees were expected to arrive formally dressed. "Gentlemen, often in great numbers, come and go, chat with each other, and act as they please," Washington once wrote of the affairs, adding, "At their *first* entrance, they salute me and I them, and as many as I can talk to I do."

Both men and women were invited to Martha's tea parties, hosted on Friday evenings. The president also attended these and circulated freely, much more at ease than at the men-only affairs.

Abigail Adams, the vice president's wife, described the president's demeanor at the parties as "polite with dignity, affable without familiarity, distant without haughtiness, grave without austerity, modest, wise, and good."

State dinners were reserved for specially invited government officials, diplomats, and other functionaries and were held on Thursdays at four o'clock. The feasts consisted of "Soup, fish, roasted and boiled meats, gammon [ham], fowls, etc. . . . The dessert was first apple pies, pudding, etc., then iced creams, jellies, etc., then watermelons, muskmelons, apples, peaches, nuts," wrote a charmed guest.

Despite the regularity and quality of the various functions that she hosted and attended weekly, Martha still had reservations about leaving the peace and tranquillity of Mount Vernon. From her new home in New York, she wrote, "I live a very dull life here and know nothing of what passes in the town. I never go to any public place. Indeed, I think I am more like a state prisoner than anything else . . . and stay home a great deal."

Soon after taking office, Washington discovered a suspicious-looking tumor on his thigh. Surgeons removed the growth and declared a complete recovery, yet the president was incapacitated for six weeks, unable to attend to any of his rapidly multiplying responsibilities. Meanwhile, during the first session of Congress, members refined the workings of the new government and defined areas not specifically covered by the Constitution, one of the most important being the designation of the various departments that would run the country. Eventually five cabinet positions were created and Washington appointed their heads: State

Department, Thomas Jefferson, fellow Virginian and minister to France; Treasury, Alexander Hamilton, a New York native, former aide, and recognized financial "genius"; War, Henry Knox, Revolutionary War stalwart from Massachusetts; Attorney General, Virginian Edmund Randolph, former delegate to the Continental Congress; and Postmaster General, Samuel Osgood, a veteran of the Revolution from Massachusetts. At the same time, he appointed John Jay of New York, who had been the secretary of foreign affairs under the old Articles of Confederation, as chief justice of the Supreme Court, along with associate justices John Rutledge of South Carolina, William Cushing of Massachusetts, Robert H. Harrison of Maryland, James Wilson of Pennsylvania, and John Blair of Virginia.

The appointments to these and many other important posts were not taken lightly by the president. He had witnessed favoritism all his life and was determined that only the best-qualified men—regardless of their social, political, or religious backgrounds—would serve the new government. He explained his feelings on the matter to a friend in May 1789, shortly after his inauguration:

> No part of my duty will be more delicate, and in many instances more unpleasing, than that of nominating or appointing persons to office. It will undoubtedly often happen that there will be several candidates for the same office, whose pretensions, ability, and integrity may be nearly equal, and who will come forward so equally supported in every respect as almost to require the aid of supernatural

intuition to fix upon the right. I shall, however, in all events, have the satisfaction to reflect that I entered upon my administration unconfined by a single engagement, uninfluenced by any ties of blood or friendship, and with the best intentions and fullest determination to nominate to office those persons only who, upon every consideration, were the most deserving, and who would probably execute their several functions to the interest and credit of the American Union.

Other important matters considered by Congress were the passage of an act to "regulate the time and manner of administering certain oaths"; tariff legislation to protect home industry; a navigation act that regulated duties based on ships' tonnage; the definition of twelve amendments to the Constitution that, upon later ratification of ten of them by the individual states, became known as the Bill of Rights; and the creation of the United States army, consisting of one infantry regiment and a battalion of artillery, a total of one thousand men.

Amid all of the frantic organizational meetings, appointments of cabinet officers, other national business, and establishment of his social calendar, Washington learned that his mother, Mary Ball Washington, had died on August 25 at age eighty-one at her home near Fredericksburg, Virginia. Although the relationship between the two had never been close, the president was nevertheless saddened. He, among all of her children, inherited the majority of her estate, thus brightening his always precarious financial standing.

———————

After more than two hundred days of hectic activity, the first session of Congress adjourned on September 29, 1789, and two weeks later the president embarked on a tour of the Northeast and New England. The trip was taken partially for "relaxation from business and reestablishment of my health," as he told his sister. It would also give him an opportunity to view a part of the country that he had not visited since the late war, he said, as well as allow him to make an assessment among the citizenry of his first five months' tenure as president.

Washington's party included his secretary, Tobias Lear, and his aide-de-camp, Major William Jackson. They traveled in a coach pulled by nine horses and attended by six servants. Luggage was conveyed in a separate wagon. On Thursday morning, October 15, Washington and his associates left the capital bound for Boston. He had last visited New England's premier city during the early days of the Revolution, when his artillerymen unleashed their sixty-hour bombardment upon its British occupiers, forcing them to evacuate. Chief Justice John Jay, Treasury Secretary Alexander Hamilton, and Secretary of War Henry Knox accompanied the party for the first few miles out of the city. Proceeding through a light rain for the rest of the day, they spent the evening at "a very neat and decent inn" at Rye, New York, having traveled thirty-one miles.

On the following day, they visited Norwalk and Fairfield, Connecticut, where "the Destructive evidences of British cruelty are yet visible . . . as there are the Chimneys of many burnt houses standing in them yet," the president recorded in his journal. New Haven, he discovered, was a thriving town of nearly four-thousand residents, with an Episcopal church, three Congregational meetinghouses, and Yale College, which supported 120 students. Upon his arrival in Boston, where he would tarry several days exploring the city, Washington was greeted with a tumultuous turnout of citizens who still revered him from his Revolutionary War generalship.

On October 28, the president visited a textile factory in Boston and was quite impressed by its output. At the same time, he made an early commentary on child labor in America. He recorded in his journal that every week the factory turned out more than one thousand yards of duck, a coarse fabric used in clothing, on twenty-eight looms operated by fourteen girls, explaining that

with Both hands (the flax being fastened to their waste. . . . Children (girls) turn the wheels for them [the looms], and with this assistance each spinner can turn out 14 lbs. of thread pr. day when they stick to it, but as they are pd. by the piece, or work they do, there is no other restraint upon them but to come at 8 Oclock in the Morning and return at 6 in the evening. They are the daughters of decayed families, and are girls of Character—none others are admitted.

From Boston, the presidential party traveled to nearby Cambridge, visiting Harvard College and its thirteen-thousand-volume library, and from there to New Hampshire and Maine—then part of Massachusetts. By November 6, the group was back in Massachusetts and, after traveling for miles through attractive countryside, but upon "amazingly crooked" roads, they reentered Connecticut. There, since it was unlawful to travel on Sundays, they rested at a tavern, "which by the bye is not a good one," the president wrote.

On November 13, after an absence of twenty-nine days, Washington arrived home in New York just as Martha was about to launch one of her weekly tea parties. He had enjoyed the leisurely journey, pleased that it had afforded him an opportunity to observe his fellow Americans at work and play and confident that his purposeful avoidance of an appearance in Rhode Island had sufficiently conveyed his displeasure to that state's officials for not yet having ratified the Constitution.

"Frequent Incursions Have Been Made on Our Frontier"

The looming issues facing Washington when he became president were the national debt, much of it left over from the Revolutionary War, and the need to reconcile citizens advocating "states' rights" with those who favored stronger, more federalized control. In the new government, the problems were interconnected. Alexander Hamilton, a financier whom the president thought could best solve the debt problem, was also a strong federalist (as were Washington and Vice President John Adams), while Thomas Jefferson, secretary of state, believed that majority power should lie with the individual states. The clash of the two strong-willed cabinet members and presidential confidants marked the beginning of the two-party system in America.

When Congress reconvened on January 4, 1790, Hamilton revealed that the country's grand total of foreign and domestic debt amounted to about fifty-six million dollars, plus another twenty-two million owed by the individual states. He urged congressmen to finance the entire debt by floating a huge bond issue, to be eventually retired with excise taxes. His proposal included the assumption of states' debts by the federal government, satisfying those states (many in the North) that still owed large sums of money but causing considerable dismay among those (primarily in the South) that had either already settled their debts or owed little. Although Washington personally favored Hamilton's proposal, including the assumption of debt, congressional leaders argued for months to no avail.

As the heat of summer grasped New York City, Hamilton confronted Jefferson in front of the new President's House, on Broad Street, and reminded him that provisions still needed to be made for the location of the permanent capital. He confided to the secretary of state that he was desperately trying to have Congress pass his debt legislation and that, if Jefferson would use his influence to help get the program implemented, he would support a movement to have the capital permanently relocated to a site along the Potomac River between Virginia and Maryland. Jefferson, anxious to have the nation's seat of government in the South, embraced Hamilton's cause, and, with his influence, Congress passed the debt proposal on August 2. Meanwhile, a bill providing for the capital's move to the Potomac within the next ten years, and its relocation to Philadelphia as a temporary site, was presented to the president for his signature on July 12. Four days later, the Residency Bill, which made the Potomac River site official, was enacted.

In August 1790, just as Congress was about to adjourn, the results of the first federal census were tallied, revealing that the new country contained 3,929,625 residents, including 697,624 slaves and 59,557 free blacks, making the total black population approximately 16 percent of the total. Virginia was the most populous state, with 747,610 inhabitants; Philadelphia, which would soon become the new temporary capital, counted a population of 42,444, making it America's largest city.

As congressmen packed their bags in preparation for recess, Washington departed for Philadelphia, where he took up official residence in the home of his old friend, Robert Morris. There he would reside until the end of his presidency and, although pleased and grateful for Morris's hospitality, he complained in a letter to Tobias Lear that while "it is, I believe, the best *single House* in the City; yet, without additions it is inadequate to the *commodious* accommodation of my family."

Leaving instructions on how to improve Morris's house to suit his own needs, President and Mrs. Washington left Philadelphia on September 6 and arrived at Mount Vernon five days later. In mid-October, Washington visited Georgetown, a small village on the Maryland side of the Potomac River, near Mount Vernon, to meet "with the principal citizens of this town and neighborhood . . . in order to fix on a proper selection for the Grand Columbian Federal City." Since the legislation authorizing the future capital mandated that it be located at a spot somewhere along an eighty-mile stretch of the Potomac, the president was immediately swamped with offers from landowners in the vicinity who realized quick profits were to be made. Following his initial survey, he returned home for a brief rest.

Two months on his beloved plantation reinvigorated him, and when he set off once again for Philadelphia in late November, he was well prepared to deliver his second annual address to Congress—one that explored the nation's complex territorial issues—on December 8. Territorial topics had always vied for the president's time and attention. Independence from Great Britain had not hastened the Crown's removal of all military personnel from common regions contested by the two countries, and several forts along the upper Mississippi River were still garrisoned by British troops. When taken into account with the Spanish prohibition against American shipping through New Orleans, they constituted a direct threat to the thousands of pioneers living in the western sections of Pennsylvania, Virginia, and North Carolina, as well as the Northwest Territory. In addition, several Indian tribes in the region looked upon these settlers' isolation, and the inability of the infant United States to respond speedily to their defensive needs, as an opportunity to wage war and regain lost ground.

On December 27, 1789, Lieutenant George Clendinen, a militiaman from Kanawha County, Virginia, and recent settler on land near Washington's own holdings, had written the president expressing a common concern:

Indians . . . have committed many hostilities, some of which, I beg leave to enumerate. They killed a man near Point Pleasant; took a young man, and a negro fellow, prisoners; have shot at others, who made their escape; and have taken between twenty and thirty head of horses. . . . If protection is not immediately given, I am sure the greater part of our frontier will be compelled to leave their homes, and either live in forts or move into the strong settled parts of the neighboring counties.

Other frontiersmen and their families experienced similar difficulties with the Indians. The western section of Virginia, which was organized into the state of Kentucky in 1792, and the Cumberland Settlements in far western North Carolina, which would become part of the state of Tennessee in 1796, had both been occupied by whites for more than a decade and had rarely experienced a peaceful moment with the numerous southern tribes. When North Carolina ceded her western holdings to the United States government in 1789 and the region fell under federal authority the following year, more woes befell the new national government as it searched for ways to protect its westward-moving population.

By September 1790, the president was anxious to make a strong statement to the hostile Indian tribes who were causing such havoc, as well as to the British and Spanish authorities who were inciting them. He dispatched General Josiah Harmar, a Revolutionary War veteran, along with a contingent of about 1,500 United States army troops and Pennsylvania and Virginia militia, from Fort Washington on the Ohio River. Near present-day Fort Wayne, Indiana, Harmar's command engaged a large party of Miami Indians, led by their chief, Little Turtle. Following a series of inglorious maneuvers by Harmar, however, the Americans were forced to retreat after suffering more than two hundred casualties.

Violence continued on the western frontier.

On January 24, 1791, Washington announced to the public that the location of the new capital would be "a part of the territory of ten miles square on both sides of the river Potomac so as to comprehend Georgetown in Maryland and to extend to the Eastern Branch." Five weeks later the District of Columbia was officially established. Also in March, Vermont entered the Union as the fourteenth state and General Arthur St. Clair, who served with Washington at Trenton and Princeton during the Revolution, was appointed commander in chief of the army, replacing the disgraced General Josiah Harmar. After meeting for only eighty-eight days, Congress adjourned its third session in early March, and on the twenty-first the president left Philadelphia, writing to his friend the marquis de Lafayette, "I shall enter on the practice of your friendly prescription of exercise, intending . . . to begin a journey to the southward, during which I propose visiting all the Southern States."

The trip carried him through Wilmington, Delaware; Annapolis and Georgetown, Maryland; Richmond, Virginia; New Bern, North Carolina; Charleston, South Carolina; and Savannah, Georgia, before reaching Augusta, Georgia, on May 18, 1791. The village of 1,100 residents, perched on the bank of the Savannah River, had become the state capital six years earlier and contained nearly three hundred dwellings, an academy with ninety students, the statehouse, a church, a courthouse, a jail, and several tobacco warehouses. The president's reception there was indicative of the pomp heaped upon him everywhere he went, each town and its people trying to outdo the other in making him welcome.

The trappings of the presidential party were spectacular. Washington's spotless white coach, pulled by four stately horses, was accompanied by a baggage wagon led by two horses, four additional saddle horses, and a military contingent that had been sent out days earlier to meet the chief executive in Savannah and escort him to Augusta. The soldiers were members of the local volunteer militia and, according to an observer, "They cut a very superb appearance . . . their uniforms being blue, faced with red and laced with silver, their caps and other accoutrements equal to their uniforms and the horses nearly of a color and in good order."

Washington was kept busy most of the following day: he participated in a review of the Augusta Volunteer Light Horse, observed a parade and an artillery salute, and attended "an elegant dinner" highlighted by fifteen toasts, among them one calling for "improvements and extension to the navigation and commerce of Georgia." On May 20 he toured plantations in the Augusta area, observed the falls of the Savannah River, and attended a private dinner party hosted by his old friend, Governor Edward Telfair, who had been a candidate in the country's first presidential election.

On May 21, Washington left his newfound friends, acquaintances, and admirers in Augusta. Thanking all of those citizens who were involved in making his stay a pleasant one, the president and his entourage crossed the Savannah River amid a final artillery salute and headed northward toward home. After stopping over at Mount Vernon for a brief visit, he reached Philadelphia on July 6 traveling, according to his own reckoning, a total of 1,887 miles. Writing to his friend Lafayette, he said that he had "been highly gratified in observing the flourishing state of the Country, and the good dispositions of the people" and that the "attachment of all Classes of citizens to the general Government seems to be a pleasing presage of their future happiness and respectability."

"Differences in Political Opinions
Are . . . Unavoidable"

The unrest on the western frontier continued throughout the summer and early fall of 1791, intensified by General Harmar's inglorious defeat the previous year by Little Turtle and his Miami tribesmen. As the first session of the Second Congress got under way, the government once again attempted to subdue the trans-Allegheny tribes. In early November 1791, General St. Clair, the new commander in chief of the army and governor of the Northwest Territory, together with 1,400 inexperienced U.S. army and Virginia militia troops, confronted Little Turtle in present-day western Ohio. They were overwhelmingly defeated by a confederation of two thousand Miami, Shawnee, Chippewa, Delaware, and Ottawa warriors. St. Clair suffered nearly nine hundred casualties in the worst defeat ever by an American army at the hands of an Indian foe. Several days later, when news of the debacle reached Washington, he was livid, declaring that St. Clair was "worst than a murderer."

By the time the president reported to Congress on December 12, he had calmed his temper: "Although the national loss is considerable . . . yet it may be repaired without great difficulty, excepting as to the brave men who have fallen on the occasion, and who are a subject of public as well as private regret."

Three days after the president addressed Congress, the Bill of Rights was ratified by legislators in Virginia, the last state vote required before the amendments would become law. Two proposed changes—to prevent congressional members from raising their salaries during the term in session, and to allow one representative for every fifty thousand residents—were universally defeated. On March 1, 1792, Thomas Jefferson announced the official results, in which ten of the twelve amendments enacted more than two years earlier became an integral part of the Constitution.

Congress adjourned on May 8 and Washington soon after left for Mount Vernon, returning to the capital in early June to learn that Kentucky had been admitted to the Union as the fifteenth state. He visited home again in July, saddened to find that his nephew and estate manager, George Augustine Washington, was dying of tuberculosis. The dread disease had infected Augustine's wife as well and, to make matters worse, malaria had stricken several slaves and servants.

One of the issues over which Washington agonized most during the early years of the republic was his inability to bring his two most trusted lieutenants to terms with each other. Thomas Jefferson, forty-nine years old in 1792, and Alexander Hamilton, fourteen years his junior, were political and philosophical opposites, yet both were valued advisers to the president, among his inner circle of confidants.

Jefferson was a graduate of the College of William and Mary, author of the Declaration of Independence, a wealthy plantation owner, and an affluent Virginia plutocrat who had already served as his state's governor and as United States minister to France. Intelligent, handsome, and a self-professed romantic, he immersed himself in the study of history, natural science, and agronomy.

His curiosity and enthusiasm were boundless. As early as 1783, when serving as a delegate in the Continental Congress, he advocated sending a government-sponsored expedition westward to discover what lay beyond the Mississippi River. A year later, as chairman of a congressional committee to study proposed statehood for the vast region north of the Ohio River, he wrote a plan that proved to be influential in the implementation of the Ordinance of 1787 creating the Northwest Territory, which eventually would be divided into the states of Ohio, Indiana, Illinois, Michigan, Wisconsin, and part of Minnesota. The classically trained Virginian suggested bestowing such exotic names as Polypotamia and Metropotamia upon the new states upon their entering the Union.

Hamilton, on the other hand, was a hard-nosed, practical businessman and attorney. Born in the West Indies and as a child deserted by his father, he migrated to America as a teenager following the death of his mother. He attended King's College in New York City but dropped out to join the Continental Army in early 1776 as a captain of artillery, serving with Washington at Trenton and Princeton and at the decisive battle at Yorktown.

Representing New York in the Continental Congress and the Annapolis Convention, Hamilton was the first to urge that a special convention be held to overhaul the inefficient Articles of Confederation. He discussed his rationale in *The Federalist Papers,* a series of pamphlets that he co-wrote supporting the proposed Constitution. He had a reputation as a financial wizard, and after Washington appointed him secretary of the treasury, he went to work attempting to reconcile the infant nation's tremendous debt and to set the country on a sound monetary footing.

The root of Jefferson's and Hamilton's differences was twofold: their strongly divided philosophies concerning the exercise of dominant American governmental power (federal versus state) and their opposite interpretations of the Constitution's intent. Jefferson believed that individual states should maintain primary responsibility for the administration of government, that federal authority must be minimal, and that the Constitution should be limited to "expressed" powers, leaving those matters not expressly covered in writing by the framers to fall within the states' jurisdictions. He and his followers, many of them southern plantation owners, were initially called "anti-Federalists" but soon adopted the name Democratic-Republicans.

Hamilton, on the other hand, advocated a strong, centralized government with only secondary powers being relinquished to the individual states. He believed that the Constitution's framers intended federal authority to be endowed with "implied" powers that would allow not only the administration of "expressed" matters, but also the control of unmentioned, or "implied," matters. Hamilton and his followers, called Federalists, were supported by many of Washington's old-time associates and much of the industrial and mercantile-based political strength of New England and the northern states.

In late August 1792, the president sent nearly identical letters to the two men, expressing his displeasure at their fierce personal antagonism and the widening political rift between them and their supporters. "How unfortunate . . . that internal dissensions should be harrowing and tearing our vitals," he wrote Jefferson. A few days later, to Hamilton, he declared, "Differences in political opinions are . . . unavoidable . . . but it is . . . to be regretted that subjects cannot be discussed with temper." In Philadelphia on October 18 he again gently chided Jefferson: "I regret, deeply regret, the difference in opinions which have arisen, and divided you and another principal Officer of the Government; and wish, devoutly, there could be an accommodation of them by mutual yieldings."

At the time Washington was writing to his disputing colleagues, the western frontier again erupted in flames. In the Cumberland Settlements, located in the newly established Territory of the United States South of the River Ohio, on land recently ceded by North Carolina, parties of Creek, Cherokee, and Shawnee Indians were maintaining a furious assault upon Nashvillians and their neighbors. In June 1792, at Ziegler's Station, located on the Cumberland twenty miles northeast of Nashville, a combined war party killed, wounded, or took prisoner a score of settlers, including seven members of one family and four of another. During the night of September 30, a Creek-Cherokee force attacked Buchanan's Station, a small fort about six miles from Nashville. Only fifteen riflemen manned the station, commanded by Major John Buchanan, who had built it a dozen years earlier. Supporting the men were their wives, who took turns casting bullets, loading rifles, and even taking up arms themselves.

Although Washington continued searching for ways to curtail the frontier violence, he remained sensitive to the fact that some of the native tribes had suffered at the hands of unscrupulous whites. When he learned in December 1792 that "certain lawless and wicked persons" in Georgia attacked and burned a Cherokee village and murdered several men and women, he angrily denounced the action, urging "all the citizens of the United States, and . . . all the officers thereof . . . to use their utmost endeavours to bring those offenders to justice," and offered a five-hundred-dollar reward for each person convicted.

News also reached Philadelphia in December that a revolutionary government had overthrown Louis XVI of France and installed a republic. Correlating the French uprising with their own bid for independence from Great Britain a decade earlier, many Americans supported the efforts of the new government. Within weeks, however, upon learning of the Reign of Terror that had seized France, and of the ruthless murder of tens of thousands of innocent French by members of the renegade government, their enthusiasm waned. King Louis and his wife, Marie-Antoinette, were eventually guillotined, along with many high-ranking members of the nobility.

Jefferson and many Democratic-Republicans were elated over the developments abroad. He had always retained a strong affinity for France and, having never personally experienced the horrors and bloodshed of war, could easily write that, for liberty's sake, he was willing to see "half the earth desolated. . . . Were there but an Adam and Eve left in every country, and left free, it would be better than it now is." The Federalists viewed the news differently. The battle-worn and war-weary president was particularly disturbed, observing that "cool reason, which alone can establish a permanent and equal government, is as little to be expected in the tumults of popular commotion as an attention to the liberties of the people is to be expected in the dark divan of a despotic tyrant."

As another presidential election loomed, Washington let it be known that he had no desire to seek a second term. Although only sixty, he told Jefferson that he was growing too old, that his memory was failing, and that "tranquility and retirement [had become] an irresistible passion." However, even his political opposites, including Jefferson himself, argued that he should accept the position once again: "North and South will hang together if they have you to hang on." Recognizing the president's extreme popularity, leaders of the Democratic-Republican Party did not oppose him.

Washington remained silent on the issue, but when state electors delivered their votes to the Electoral College for ratification in early February 1793, he was unanimously reelected, and his running mate, John Adams, was returned to office as well.

"We . . . Cannot Deny . . . the Right Whereon Our Own Government Is Founded"

On January 20, 1793, even before the election results were officially tallied in Philadelphia, Washington wrote a longtime friend, Virginia governor Henry Lee, "A mind must be insensible indeed, not to be gratefully impressed by so distinguished, & honorable a testimony of public approbation & confidence." He added a note of sadness since, once again, he would be carried away from Mount Vernon and the life he loved: "To say I feel pleasure from the prospect of *commencing* another tour of duty, would be a departure from truth."

The inauguration was held at noon on March 4, 1793, and its formality and solemnity were in stark contrast to the first gala ceremony four years earlier. Since no precedent existed for a president succeeding himself in office, Washington conferred with his cabinet and decided to keep the affair as simple and informal as possible. At the appointed time, he left home alone in a carriage that took him to the senate chambers, where he recited the shortest inaugural address ever given by an American president:

> I am again called upon by the voice of my country to execute the functions of its Chief Magistrate. When the occasion proper for it shall arrive, I shall endeavor to express the high sense I entertain of this distinguished honor, and of the confidence which has been reposed in me by the people of united America.
>
> Previous to the execution of any official act of the President the Constitution requires an oath of office. This oath I am now about to take, and in your presence: That if it shall be found during my administration of the Government I have in any instance violated willingly or knowingly the injunctions thereof, I may (besides incurring constitutional punishment) be subject to the upbraidings of all who are now witnesses of the present solemn ceremony.

He then repeated the brief oath of office administered by Supreme Court Associate Justice William Cushing and, after shaking hands and exchanging pleasantries with the small gathering of well-wishers, went back to work.

Most of the troublesome issues with which Washington and his cabinet had labored during the first administration had resisted resolution and faced the president as he began his second term. Jefferson and Hamilton, both of whom retained their cabinet positions, were still bickering in public and in private as the chasm between the Federalists and the Democratic-Republicans grew wider. News from France soon revealed that Louis XVI and other members of his court had been guillotined, that the monarchy had been replaced by the "Republic of France," and that a political purge was in the offing. The trans-Allegheny Indian tribes and white settlers had solved few of the issues confronting them as the frontier moved rapidly westward.

And there were personal problems. Washington received news from Mount Vernon in early February that his nephew and farm manager, George Augustine Washington, ill for several months, had died, leaving the estate without a responsible overseer. The president hired a new manager and soon began inundating him with correspondence, well sprinkled with advice about everything from what to pay for spring wheat to an admonition to save all of the orchard grass seed possible (since having to purchase it "is an intolerable expense"), and from misgivings over how six thousand nails could be required for repairing a corn crib to a concern for one of the servants. "Sarah Flatfoot (you call her Lightfoot) has been accustomed to receive a pair of Shoes, Stockings, a Country cloth Petticoat, & an Oznabrig shift, all ready made, annually, & it is not meant to discontinue them: you will therefore furnish them to her."

Although dissension among Washington's highest-ranking officials, particularly Jefferson and Hamilton, continued to aggravate him, he now faced an even larger issue that would require all of his diplomatic skills. As news regarding the volatile situation in France continued to arrive, it became clear to him that he must maintain United States neutrality toward the new French republic; to do otherwise would infuriate Great Britain, with whom relations were already tenuous. Yet a vast majority of Americans supported the radical movement abroad, still relating it to their own recent struggles with Great Britain; even Washington, personally, sympathized with the country that had helped him so much during the war with England.

He warned that the causes of the French upheaval were far different from those that sparked the American Revolution. The French revolt was an internal one and had occurred when the country's common people rebelled against the excesses of the Crown, causing large sectors of the populace to band together and depose Louis XVI. When their mission was accomplished, the factions then turned upon each other, making it only a matter of time before France was engulfed in bloodshed, with the original goals of the rebellion forgotten. Meantime, France declared war on England, making matters more complicated than ever.

As expected, the secretaries of state and of the treasury stood opposed on the issue. Jefferson, a passionate Francophile, along with his Democratic-Republican followers, urged Washington to lend immediate American support to the uprising, calling it a fight for "liberty, fraternity and equality." Hamilton and the Federalists termed the revolt a cauldron of "atheism, depravity and absurdity" and were just as adamant in their demands that France not be accorded special treatment. Finally, the president, rationalizing that "we surely cannot deny to any nation the right whereon our own government is founded, that every nation may govern itself according to whatever form it pleases," allowed Jefferson to recognize the revolutionary government, while still expressing doubts about taking sides in the conflict.

On April 18, 1793, Washington sent identical letters to his cabinet members in which he posed thirteen detailed questions about the French quandary, ranging from "Shall a Minister from the Republic of France be received?" to "Is it necessary, or advisable, to call together the two Houses of Congress, with a view to the present posture of European affairs?" When the questions and their answers were discussed with the cabinet the following day, the president overrode Jefferson's objections and decided that the United States should remain neutral, while allowing that it was proper for a French minister to be received. Accordingly, three days later, he issued a Proclamation of Neutrality in which he advised the combatants, which now included Austria, Prussia, and Sardinia on Great Britian's side versus France, that America would "with sincerity and good faith adopt and pursue a conduct friendly and impartial towards [all] the belligerent powers."

Had Washington and the rest of the country's officialdom known the trouble that the new French minister would cause, they might have had second thoughts about their decision. In fact, he had already arrived in Charleston, South Carolina, on April 8, two weeks before the president issued his Proclamation of Neutrality. Edmond Charles Edouard Genêt, self-styled "Citizen" Genêt, a cocky, self-assured commoner who had landed his position simply by being a follower of his country's revolutionary movement, breached the rules of diplomacy when he failed to proceed directly to Philadelphia and officially present himself to the president. Instead, he spent six weeks in the South, illegally attempting to recruit an American army to march on Spanish-held Louisiana, and conferring with local shipbuilders about outfitting a fleet of warships with which privateers could raid British shipping on the high seas.

Soon after Genêt finally appeared before Washington, to a somewhat cool reception, he was informed that he had overstepped his authority, that his actions in Charleston were illegal, and that any vessels already commissioned must leave United States waters at once. The Frenchman balked, angrily replying that, regardless of the president's orders, he intended to place the matter before the American people for consideration before revoking his plans. The diplomat's audacity shocked even Jefferson, who wrote to the American minister in Paris requesting Genêt's recall. By February 1794, a new regime had gained government control in France and a new minister, Baron Jean Antoine Joseph Fauchet, whom Martha Washington described as "a plain, grave, and good man," arrived in Philadelphia, replacing Genêt and authorizing the "Citizen's" arrest and return to France. Washington, always kind, even to his enemies, denied the extradition order, and Genêt eventually married the daughter of New York governor George Clinton and lived the rest of his life in relative obscurity.

During the summer of 1793, amid a virulent yellow fever epidemic in Philadelphia, Washington and his family vacationed in Mount Vernon. In September, he journeyed to the site of the new capital on the Potomac River, where construction on the President's House was proceeding frantically and work on other public buildings was about to begin. On September 18, surrounded by members of Alexandria's Masonic Lodge 22, of which he had once served as Worshipful Master, he supervised the laying of the cornerstone to the Capitol. The ceremony was a grand affair, with a parade, cannon salutes, music, and a giant barbecue supper. The *Alexandria Gazette* reported, "The ceremony ended in prayer, Masonic chanting Honours, and a fifteen [gun] volley from the Artillery" and that, as darkness approached, "the whole company departed with joyful hopes of the production of their labor."

As 1793 came to a close, Jefferson announced that he would leave the cabinet at the end of December. Although the two men had their differences, the president reluctantly accepted the decision, wondering how he could ever replace his fellow Virginian. Washington biographer James Thomas Flexner wrote, "Jefferson's retirement was undoubtedly the greatest catastrophe Washington suffered during his Presidency. . . . The very essence of Washington's decision-making process was set awry . . . [because] he endeavored, before he reached a conclusion, to balance all points of view. . . . Now, when Hamilton spoke, there was no equally strong voice to answer."

Realistically, other matters confronted by the president during his eight-year administration were equally critical but, with Jefferson's resignation, the nation lost diplomatic and philosophical skills difficult to replace.

"A Mission Like This . . . Will Announce . . . Solicitude for Friendly Adjustment"

To replace Jefferson as secretary of state, Washington selected Attorney General Edmund Randolph, a forty-year-old Virginia lawyer, former governor of the state, and aide-de-camp to the president during the Revolution. Although Jefferson and Randolph were cousins, the former secretary had little respect for his kinsman, labeling him wavering and a "mere chameleon" and declaring that Washington could not have made a more unfortunate appointment.

As the new year, 1794, got under way, however, the president had more important matters on his mind than the continuous turmoil within his cabinet. The British government had recently issued the Provision Order which, in its broadest terms, allowed the Crown's navy to board, search, and impound American ships suspected of trading with the French or entering and leaving French ports. Since a great deal of American commerce was pursued in the French West Indies, scores of ships were seized, their cargoes confiscated, and their crews forced either to join the British navy or submit to arrest.

Meanwhile, the British were once again inciting the Indian tribes in the Northwest Territory and creating rumors that war was imminent between England and the United States. Washington lamented to a friend, "If, instead of the provocation to war, bloodshed, and desolation . . . the strife of nations and individuals was to excel each other in acts of philanthropy, industry, and economy, in encouraging useful arts and manufactures, promoting thereby the comfort and happiness of our fellow men . . . how much happier would mankind be!"

In mid-April 1794, in an attempt to resolve the lingering issues, Washington proposed to the Senate that a special envoy be sent to London:

> A mission like this, while it corresponds with the solemnity of the occasion, will announce to the world a solicitude for friendly adjustment. . . . Going immediately from the United States, such an envoy will carry with him knowledge of the existing temper and sensibility of the country, and will thus be taught to vindicate our rights with firmness, and to cultivate peace with sincerity.

Federalist factions wanted Hamilton to be the envoy, while the Democratic-Republicans, fearful that the treasury secretary would unfairly represent their affiliations with France, strongly dissented. Federalists themselves solved the impasse by persuading the eager Hamilton to withdraw his name from consideration, replacing it with that of Supreme Court chief justice John

Jay. Shortly thereafter, the president dispatched Jay, with a valise full of instructions, to London to hammer out a lasting treaty with the Crown.

The president traveled to his plantation in early July 1794 to take care of personal business and hire a new manager after the unexpected death of his overseer. "My concerns at Mt. Vernon are left as a body without a head," Washington wrote to his friend Governor Henry Lee. By the time he returned to Philadelphia on July 12, another crisis had arisen.

In 1791 Congress had levied a tax on domestically manufactured whiskey. To the farmers in western Pennsylvania, the tax was particularly offensive since it was far more economical to distill their grain into whiskey than to transport it laboriously to market across miles of wilderness. Affairs had rocked along until July, when a federal marshal was attacked while serving legal papers on a local distiller and, in a separate incident, a tax inspector's house was burned. When a number of other outrages occurred against federal officials in the area, Washington sought advice from his cabinet officers about the proper course of action to take in the so-called Whiskey Rebellion. Treasury Secretary Hamilton called the acts treasonous and demanded immediate reprisals, while Secretary of State Randolph advocated a softer stance, fearing that the rebels might adopt an even more hostile position.

On August 7, after assessing his associates' advice, Washington issued a lengthy proclamation authorizing the militia of any state to be called out "whenever the laws of the United States shall be opposed or the execution of them obstructed in any State by combinations too powerful to be suppressed by the ordinary course of judicial proceedings." Moreover, the order demanded that by September 1 the insurgents in Washington and Allegheny Counties, Pennsylvania, where most of the rebellion was taking place, desist from their "treasonable acts" and disband, or suffer the consequences. When the deadline to disperse passed and reports reached Philadelphia that the tax protesters were still disrupting the peace, the president issued a second proclamation, on September 25, in which he announced that militiamen from Pennsylvania, New Jersey, Maryland, and Virginia had been activated "to reduce the refractory to a due subordination of the law."

Five days later, the president left the capital to rendezvous and take command of an army larger than any he had organized during the Revolutionary War. In early October he met with representatives of the rebelling counties and departed, believing that in view of the army's show of force a peaceful resolution would soon be forthcoming. Leaving Virginia governor Henry Lee in command, he returned to Philadelphia. By late November, the Whiskey Rebellion ended with minimal bloodshed and the dispersal of the militia, leaving Washington satisfied once again that the philosophy and strength of the Federalist faction had prevailed, and that, had the individual states been left alone to address the problem, the outcome might have been disastrous.

During the summer and fall of 1794, while John Jay labored in London with British officials over new treaty provisions that would restore some semblance of peace between the Crown and the United States, and while Washington attempted to defuse the Whiskey Rebellion, affairs on the western frontier reached an impasse.

In the Northwest Territory, General Anthony Wayne, who had succeeded Arthur St. Clair as commander of the army in 1792, had been training a three-thousand-man force for over a year to punish Little Turtle's confederation of warriors for its earlier defeats of Generals Harmar and St. Clair. Following a skirmish with Wayne on June 29, in which he was intimidated by the strength of the American troops, Little Turtle urged his lieutenants to sue for peace. He was replaced by Turkey Foot, a recalcitrant chief who in August confronted Wayne's army along the Maumee River at a place called Fallen Timbers, near present-day Toledo, Ohio. Within two hours, the Indians suffered a decisive defeat, losing hundreds of warriors to Wayne's thirty-three killed and one hundred wounded.

The Americans proceeded to raid the entire area, destroying villages and burning five thousand acres of cropland in a fury from which the Indian confederation never fully recovered. In a message to Congress three months later, Washington proudly proclaimed that General Wayne's victory was "a happy presage to our military operations against the hostile Indians, north of the Ohio," and that it "must have damped the ardor of the savages, and weakened their obstinacy in waging war against the United States."

In early September, Indian affairs in the Southwest Territory climaxed as well. Despite the president's admonition to residents of the Cumberland Settlements to refrain from invading the

Cherokee homeland, General James Robertson, founder of Nashville, ordered a local force of 550 mounted infantry under the command of Major James Ore to attack two Indian towns, Nickajack and Running Water, located along the Tennessee River. Upwards of fifty tribesmen were killed and twenty more were carried back to Nashville as prisoners. In the official report to Territorial Governor William Blount, Major Ore explained the importance of the invasion:

> The Running Water was counted the largest, and among the most hostile towns of the Cherokees. Nickajack was not less hostile, but inferior in point of numbers. At Nickajack was found two fresh scalps, which had lately been taken at Cumberland, and several that were old were hanging in the houses of the warriors, as trophies of war; a quantity of ammunition, powder, and lead, lately arrived there from the Spanish Government, and a commission for the Breath, the head-man of the town, who was killed, and sundry horses, and other articles of property, were found, both at Nickajack and the Running Water, which were known by one or other of the militia to have belonged to different people, killed by Indians, in the course of the last twelve months.

The overwhelming successes in subduing the hostile tribes in both the Northwest and the Southwest marked the beginning of a lull in native aggression toward white settlement in the two regions. There would be a few years of relative peace west of the Alleghenies until, during the War of 1812, once again instigated in part by British machinations, the tribes would make one last effort to expel the Americans.

Although Washington did not learn of it for some weeks, the treaty forged with Great Britain by John Jay was signed on November 19, 1794. Among other provisions, it called for British withdrawal from the Northwest Territory by June 1, 1796; unrestricted American shipping privileges to the British East Indies; settlement of nearly three million dollars of American debt from the late war with England; and United States acceptance of British trade on a most-favored-nation basis. An article that allowed provisional American shipping privileges to the British West Indies (excluding trade in sugar, molasses, and cotton) was stricken before Senate approval. Issues not addressed were Britain's involvement in the frontier Indian problems, its illegal seizure of American ships, and the impressment of American seamen.

When the treaty was submitted to the Senate for ratification the following spring, it was met with mixed emotion, primarily along party lines, with Federalists generally favoring it and Democratic-Republicans denouncing it as unfair to France. After lengthy debate, assisted by considerable behind-the-scenes lobbying by both factions, it was ratified on June 24, 1795.

"I Have, with Good Intentions, Contributed Towards the . . . Government"

As 1795 opened, Washington was faced with more cabinet resignations. Timothy Pickering, the forty-nine-year-old former quartermaster general of the Continental Army, and most recently postmaster general, replaced Henry Knox as secretary of war. On January 31 Alexander Hamilton, the man whose opinions the president valued most, left his post as secretary of the treasury, to be succeeded by Oliver Wolcott, Jr., son of a signer of the Declaration of Independence who had served under General Horatio Gates at Saratoga. Of those the president selected for his first cabinet nearly six years earlier, only Edmund Randolph remained, now as secretary of state.

In July, Washington reached Mount Vernon, "after a hot and disagreeable ride." Although Jay's treaty had been ratified the previous month, the final language still remained to be adopted due to the Senate's deletion of the section concerning West Indian trade. Now the president had doubts whether the treaty would ever be totally supported by the American people. "At present the cry against [it] is like that against a mad-dog; and every one, in a manner, seems engaged in running it down," he wrote to Hamilton, with whom he still maintained a vigorous correspondence.

His stay in Virginia was cut short upon receiving a letter signed by Secretary of War Timothy Pickering urging him to return to Philadelphia at once. Upon his arrival on August 11, he was mortified to learn that his faithful friend and personal lawyer, Edmund Randolph, the secretary of state, was suspected by his fellow cabinet members of committing treasonous acts against the United States during the Whiskey Rebellion. Based on a letter written a year earlier, Pickering, Oliver Wolcott, and William Bradford, who had succeeded Randolph as attorney general, accused the secretary of offering, for a price, to intervene in the rebellion on behalf of some antigovernment protesters.

Alone that night in the President's House, Washington grew depressed as he read the lengthy indicting letter. On another occasion, fifteen years earlier, he had experienced the same sickening feeling when he learned that his old friend General Benedict Arnold had offered to surrender West Point to the British. Now, it appeared that another confidant had betrayed his country in exchange for monetary gain.

Several days later, in the presence of Wolcott and Pickering, the president confronted Randolph with the letter. Watching the secretary's facial expression as he read the document, the others were surprised when he showed no emotion, but rather acted "with composure." Washington interpreted Randolph's reaction to signify innocence, but when he started to speak, Randolph, shaken by the apparent lack of confidence among his associates, blurted out that he "could not continue in the office one second after such treatment" and stormed out of the room.

The secretary later wrote to a friend, "I feel happy at my emancipation from attachment to a man who has practiced on me the profound hypocrisy of a Tiberius and the injustice of an assassin." In the months to come, he produced documents that seemed to refute his perceived guilt, but by then it was too late. The close relationship with the president was over and his reputation had been severely tarnished. Several years later he suffered a stroke which left him paralyzed. He died, bedridden and in agony, in 1813. Ironically, Washington selected one of his accusers, Timothy Pickering, to succeed him as secretary of state.

Although a fact perhaps not appreciated at the time, the signing and ratification of Jay's treaty provided the United States with the means it needed to resolve the last of its problems with Spain: the possession and control of the lower Mississippi River valley. Following the Revolution, Great Britain had ceded its Florida provinces to Spain, which recognized the boundary between its newly acquired territory and the United States to be one hundred miles farther north than the American claim. Refusing to relinquish the contested region, Spain thus controlled both banks of the lower Mississippi River, denying American merchants and farmers access to the marketplaces of New Orleans. The problem was hardly new and had been responsible for

Washington's keen interest years earlier in completing a canal network from the Atlantic to the trans-Allegheny region.

The situation was especially critical for the federal government since settlers in Kentucky and the Southwest Territory had, for years, seriously considered severing relations with the United States and forming a coalition with Spain. A Spanish-American state would remedy the settlers' need for ready access to markets and provide badly needed military support. (Many westerners were infuriated over the inability of the federal government to defend the far frontier against Indian raids.)

Upon receiving news of Jay's treaty, Spanish diplomats feared that the pact signified renewed friendship and cooperation between the United States and England, with whom they were about to declare war, and so made overtures to Washington that they were interested in negotiating a settlement of the years-long issues. Thomas Pinckney, the former governor of South Carolina and currently the United States minister to England, was immediately dispatched to Spain. There, in October 1795, he crafted an agreement that satisfied the United States on virtually every point of contention: the opening of the Mississippi River to western merchants and farmers, the recognition of its claim along Spanish Florida's northern border, and tighter control over the Indians who maintained villages in Spanish-held territory.

Early in 1796, Washington decided that his advancing age (he was approaching sixty-four), his failing health, and the growing burden of his landholdings provided compelling reasons to refuse a third presidential term. "[I will] close my public life on March 4 [1797], after which no consideration under heaven that I can foresee shall again draw me from the walks of private life," he wrote to Alexander Hamilton. He would personally manage his Mount Vernon estate, now consisting of five separate divisions—the Mansion, the River, the Union, the Muddy Hole, and the Dogue Farms—each operated independently with its own staff of slaves, workmen, and servants, and each maintaining its own animal herds, dwellings, barns, dairy, and smokehouses.

In February 1796, he placed advertisements in several American and English newspapers proposing to lease for fall occupancy all of the farms except the Mansion House "for the term of fourteen years to *real* farmers of *good* reputation, and none others need apply." Considering his love for the plantation and his longing to be back in Virginia among family, friends, and employees, he probably was not disappointed when none of the advertisement's respondents qualified as a potential lessee.

Washington's last full year in office witnessed the enactment of several pieces of important legislation. In April, in a wide-ranging effort to bring America's native population into line with the ever-growing white presence on the frontier, Congress passed "An Act for Establishing Trading-Houses with the Indian Tribes," for the purpose "of carrying on a liberal trade with the several Indian nations within the limits of the United States." The Factory System, eventually numbering twenty-eight houses, each one manned by a civilian factor, had been discussed as early as 1776 when the Continental Congress had unsuccessfully considered a version of the plan. Not until 1795, however, were sufficient funds—fifty thousand dollars—appropriated for the purchase of trade goods with which to stock the first two houses located among the Cherokee, Creek, and Chickasaw tribes.

In May, the nation's first wildlife protection law, delineating specific hunting seasons for game, was enacted, and an important treaty with the Six Nations of the Iroquois was signed. On June 1, 1796, Tennessee was admitted to the Union as the sixteenth state. In August, Washington sent a lengthy memorial to the leaders of the Cherokee tribe in which he admonished them to replace their native lifestyles with those of the white people so that they "might enjoy in abundance all the good things which make life comfortable and happy" and to "raise live stock not only for your own wants, but to sell."

In his farewell address, dated September 19, which he did not deliver in person to Congress, he pleaded with all Americans to be wary of permanent foreign alliances, to protect the country's hard-won credit, and avoid the creation of political parties (although, in reality, the two-party system was already in operation). Finally, he wrote:

I have, with good intentions, contributed towards the Organization and Administration of the government, the best exertions of which a very fallible judgment was capable. Not unconscious in the outset, of the inferiority of my qualifications, experience in my own eyes, perhaps still more in the eyes of others, has strengthened the motives to diffidence of myself; and every day the encreasing weight of years admonishes me more and more, that the shade of retirement is as necessary to me as it will be welcome.

THE VIRGINIA DYNASTY

The Commonwealth of Virginia has furnished an unprecedented eight men to the presidency of the United States, more than any other state in the Union. Four of the first five chief executives were born there, and for thirty-two years of the country's first five decades of nationhood, Virginians held executive power. During that first half-century, the very foundations of the United States government—the political structure and institutions that are taken so much for granted today—were established and implemented.

George Washington was the first Virginian to serve, followed by Thomas Jefferson, James Madison, and James Monroe, the third, fourth, and fifth presidents, respectively. The era covered by the terms of these four men has been called "the Virginia Dynasty." The remaining four Virginia presidents were William Henry Harrison, John Tyler, Zachary Taylor, and Woodrow Wilson.

The four presidents included in the Virginia Dynasty, along with some of the history-making events that occurred during their administrations, are as follows:

GEORGE WASHINGTON (1732–1799) was, without question, the most famous man in America when he was elected to the presidency of the new nation in 1789. Born in Westmoreland County, the hero of the Revolution had for more than six years successfully guided the fledgling American army to victory over Britain's elite fighting machine, culminating with his defeat of Lord Cornwallis at Yorktown, Virginia, in October 1781. While in office from 1789 to 1797, President Washington witnessed the invention of the cotton gin, a feat that had monumental effects on the predominately agricultural South. Other important events occurring during his administration were the relocation of the nation's capital from New York to Philadelphia, the founding of the New York Stock Exchange, and America's first successful flight of a hot-air balloon.

THOMAS JEFFERSON (1743–1826) was already well known before he served as the country's third president, 1801–1809. He was born in Albemarle County and when in his early thirties became the principal author of the Declaration of Independence. Jefferson also was secretary of state in George Washington's first administration, as well as vice president to President John Adams. During his two terms as president, Jefferson vastly expanded the size of the United States by his purchase of the Louisiana Territory from France in 1803 and provided the inspiration for the Lewis and Clark Expedition from St. Louis to the Pacific Ocean and back from 1804 to 1806. Following his presidency, he helped establish the University of Virginia, provided his book collection for the cornerstone of the Library of Congress collection, and maintained his plantation at Monticello.

Jefferson's successor was JAMES MADISON (1751–1836), who served as president from 1809 to 1817. The "father" of the United States Constitution and a founder of the Democratic-Republican Party, he was born in King George County. America's second war with England took place during Madison's terms in office, and he and his wife, Dolley, witnessed the burning of the capital. Two significant milestones in science occurred during his presidency. In Kentucky, Dr. Ephraim McDowell removed an ovarian tumor from Mrs. Jane Crawford, who tolerated the thirty-minute operation, the world's first ovariotomy, without anesthesia. And the rapid development of the steam engine allowed the first successful navigation of the Mississippi River by steamboat.

JAMES MONROE (1758–1831), the nation's fifth president, was born in Westmoreland County and served two terms, from 1817 to 1825, during a period sometimes referred to as "the era of good feeling" due to his strong and successful administration. Monroe expanded the size of the United

States by the purchase of Spanish Florida, established an unarmed U.S.-Canadian border which persists to this day, and oversaw the passage of the Missouri Compromise. The achievement for which he will always be remembered, however, was his enactment of the Monroe Doctrine, which defiantly proclaimed to the world that the countries of the Western Hemisphere "are henceforth not to be considered as subjects for future colonization by any European powers."

"Everything We Hold Dear and Sacred [Is] . . . Seriously Threatened"

Washington delivered his last public address to Congress on December 7, 1796, declaring, "The situation in which I now stand, for the last time . . . naturally recalls the period when the administration of the present form of government commenced; and I cannot omit the occasion to congratulate you, and my country, on the success of the experiment; nor to repeat my fervent supplication to the Supreme Ruler of the universe and Sovereign Arbiter of nations, that his providential care may still be extended to the United States."

For the forthcoming election, the Federalists selected John Adams as their presidential candidate and Thomas Pinckney for the vice presidency. Democratic-Republicans chose Thomas Jefferson and Aaron Burr to head their ticket. The president took no part in the process and made a special effort to show no favoritism among candidates. When the electoral votes were tallied in Philadelphia in February 1797, Adams received seventy-one, and Jefferson sixty-eight, making the political opposites the president-elect and vice president-elect, respectively.

On Friday, March 3, his concluding day in office, Washington commuted the sentences of ten men who had been convicted of treason during the Whiskey Rebellion. In his last letter as president, he wrote to Jonathan Trumbull, a wartime aide-de-camp and former speaker of the House of Representatives, "Although I shall resign the chair of government without a single regret, or any desire to intermeddle in politics again, yet there are many of my compatriots (among whom be assured I place you) from whom I shall depart sorrowing; because, unless I meet with them at Mount Vernon it is not likely that I shall ever see them more, as I do not expect that I shall ever be twenty miles from it after I am tranquilly settled there." Despite this being the last evening that he and Martha would spend together as President and Mrs. Washington, the only entry in his diary for the day simply noted that the temperature had climbed to 34 degrees and that the wind had blown out of the southwest.

The following day, he attended the inauguration before a joint session of Congress in Federal Hall. He was attired in a well-worn black frock coat, in contrast to the new president's gray, tailor-made suit. Although the two men shared practically identical political philosophies and Adams was responsible for propelling Washington onto the national scene nearly twenty years earlier by nominating him for commander in chief of the Continental Army, the new president looked upon his predecessor as an uneducated boor. Even so, in his inaugural address, Adams wished for Washington a long life "to enjoy the delicious recollection of his services [and] the gratitude of mankind," and proclaimed, "His name may be still a rampart, and the knowledge that he lives a bulwark against all open or secret enemies of this country's peace."

Now private citizens, the Washingtons remained in the Philadelphia area for a few days, visiting old friends, attending going-away dinners, and arranging for a ship to transport to Mount Vernon selected pieces of furniture, art, and household items—in all, two hundred boxes. On the morning of March 9, the entourage—including Martha's granddaughter, Nelly, and George Washington Lafayette, the marquis's son, who was visiting together with his tutor—began the journey for Virginia. As the horse-drawn coach prepared to depart the city, the happy former president kept busy with a myriad of details, proclaiming that he was even "called upon to remember the parrot . . . [and] the dog," but that "for my own part, I should not pine if they were both forgot."

After nearly a week of wearisome travel that included festive dinners and receptions in Baltimore, Georgetown, the District of Columbia, and Alexandria, Washington's party arrived at Mount Vernon. The president had walked around the grounds and surveyed the mansion house for only a few minutes when he realized that, despite the efforts of a long line of caring overseers, including his own cousin and nephew, the plantation clearly showed the effects of nearly a decade of neglect and that much effort and expense would be required to restore it to its past splendor.

Within two weeks of arriving home, Washington had so many workmen on site replacing decayed structures, repairing mantels and steps, and painting inside and out that he could scarcely spare "a room to put a friend into or set in myself without the music of hammers or the odoriferous smell of paint." His years of holding positions of power were hard to forget as he demanded promptness from his workers, writing to a friend, "If my hirelings are not in their places at that time [dawn], I send them messages expressive of my sorrow for their indisposition."

His time was fully occupied, causing him to complain to a friend, "I have not looked into a Book since I came home, nor shall I be able to do it until I have discharged my Workmen." A typical day consisted of having breakfast at seven, then riding over the five farms on horseback, returning to the mansion in "time to dress for dinner at which I rarely miss seeing strange faces, come as they say out of respect for me," taking a brief walk followed by tea, and finally retiring to his writing table to answer letters.

His depression over the run-down condition of Mount Vernon was deepened when he was visited by Richard Parkinson, author of a popular book, *The Experienced Farmer,* and a renowned British agronomist. The Englishman had responded to one of the advertisements offering to lease parts of the plantation that had run in several newspapers during the president's last weeks in Philadelphia. Although Washington was well aware that the soil quality of all of his farms along the Potomac was poor and that its thinness contributed heavily to severe erosion, he was dismayed when Parkinson, "with a great deal of frankness," criticized every aspect of the estate, from poor crop yields to animal inferiority, and cited "strong proofs of his mistakes." He found little solace in the fact that, despite the expert's condemnation of practically everything else, he revered the Mount Vernon mules.

During the winter of 1797–98, Washington learned from correspondence with former cabinet members that American affairs with France had badly deteriorated and that President Adams had dispatched a three-man delegation to Paris to attempt to resolve the two countries' issues. After being introduced to the Americans, the French foreign minister refused to meet with them again, assigning the negotiations to subordinates who suggested that a large bribe, along with an even larger loan, would go a long way toward solving the problems. When, later in the spring, news of the debacle reached the United States, most Americans adopted an anti-French attitude.

In May 1798, anticipating possible war with France, Alexander Hamilton, who had maintained some influence with President Adams, wrote to Washington suggesting "In the event of an open rupture with France, the public voice will again call you to command the armies of your Country." The former president quickly responded that he doubted France would risk an all-out war with America, but said, "If a crisis should arrive when a sense of duty, or a call from my Country should become so imperious as to leave me no Choice I should prepare for the relinquishment & go with as much reluctance from my present peaceful abode, as I should do to the tombs of my ancestors."

He was much disturbed on an early July day when he received simultaneous letters from the president and secretary of war, both asking him to assume command of all the armies. A few days later, he sent Adams his reply. He said that at a time in history when "everything we hold dear and sacred [is] so seriously threatened, I have finally determined to accept the Commission of Commander in Chief of the Armies of the United States," with the proviso that he not be called "into the field until the Army is in a situation to require my presence, or it becomes indispensable by the urgency of circumstances."

He selected three men with the rank of major general to serve with his command: Alexander Hamilton, former secretary of war Henry Knox, and former minister to France Charles Cotesworth Pinckney. Knox turned down the offer, instead opting for the role as Washington's aide-de-camp if war ever came. The regular army was increased to ten thousand men, to be supplemented by a fifty-thousand-man "provisional army." The one bright aspect of the entire situation occurred when President Adams assured Washington that his position qualified him for a secretary. On August 30, the commander wrote to his old friend and former employee Tobias Lear, who years before had become involved in private business in the District of Columbia, "I should be glad if you would now come & take your station."

In November, Washington traveled to Philadelphia to confer about army matters with Hamilton and Pinckney, to devise plans on recruiting the new army, select officers, and assign commands. Upon arriving home in December, he continued his role as master of Mount Vernon but kept in constant communication with his peers in Philadelphia.

Winter passed without a great deal of news from the capital about either the French threat or the organizational progress of the army. That Secretary of War James McHenry demonstrated little interest or intent in revitalizing the army according to the plans submitted by Washington, Hamilton, and Pinckney was particularly troublesome to the three generals. In late March 1799, Washington wrote a lengthy, detailed letter to McHenry, accusing him of missing the opportunity early in the French crisis to recruit quality officers and men eager to don the uniform. "What is the natural consequence of all this?" he asked. "Why, that we must take the Rif-raf of the populous Cities; Convicts; & foreigners; or, have Officers without men." He closed his letter with an uncharacteristic attack on the secretary's competence, writing that he had been told "in pretty *strong terms* by more than one . . . that the Department of War would not—nay could not—be conducted to advantage (if War should ensue) under your auspices." He revealed that while the secretary's staff kept "rigidly to their respective duties . . . you . . . were bewildered with trifles."

Washington's remonstrance had little effect on McHenry, and affairs in the War Department continued to deteriorate. By summer, the regular army had processed only three thousand additional recruits, and the huge "provisional" army had never been seriously considered beyond the planning stage. The French crisis was quieted, at least for a time, and Washington once again turned his attention toward home.

"Let Me Go Off Quietly;
I Cannot Last Long"

On July 9, 1799, Washington sat down at his desk in the study at Mount Vernon and wrote his last will and testament. It was a lengthy document, of more than five thousand words, and in it the weary Virginian waxed eloquent as he made arrangements for a vast number of bequests to family and friends.

To Martha he left the "use, profit and, benefit of my whole Estate, real and personal, for the term of her natural life," excluding specific items that he designated for other individuals. He decreed that upon Martha's death, "It is my Will and desire that all the Slaves which I hold in *my own right,* shall receive their freedom," explaining that to "emancipate them during [her] life, would, tho' earnestly wished by me, be attended with . . . insuperable difficulties" with the slaves Martha owned and had brought into the marriage and over whom he had no control. He left instructions for clothing, feeding, and educating young orphan slaves, and expressly forbade the "Sale, or transportation out of said Commonwealth [Virginia], of any Slave I may die possessed of, under any pretense whatsoever." And, to William Lee, an elderly mulatto slave who had been with Washington for many years, he bestowed "immediate freedom" and a gift of thirty dollars, "as a testimony of my sense of his attachment to me, and for his faithful services during the Revolutionary War."

Washington had a sizable number of blood relatives and close friends and, to each of them, and to many of Martha's kin as well, he willed some item of value, from building lots in the District of Columbia to his other farms along the Potomac, and from the gold-headed walking stick given to him by Benjamin Franklin to a pair of "finely wrought steel Pistols." To his faithful secretary, Tobias Lear, he gave the use of a 360-acre farm, free of rent, until Lear's death. To each of his five nephews he left one of his valuable swords, "with an injunction not to unsheath them for the purpose of shedding blood, except it be for self defence, or in defence of their Country and its rights."

When he had finished writing, Washington had disposed of his entire estate, conservatively valued at well over half a million dollars. His landholdings alone numbered more than thirty-three thousand acres in states ranging from Virginia to New York and Kentucky, as well as the Northwest Territory. Stocks held in various entities, including those early canal companies in which he had a hand in organizing, totaled more than twenty-five thousand dollars, while the livestock at Mount Vernon and its neighboring farms along the Potomac was valued at $15,653.

Mount Vernon had never ceased to be a center of activity. Washington had once written to a friend, "Unless someone pops in, unexpectedly—Mrs. Washington and myself will do what I believe has not been done within the last twenty years by us—that is to set down to dinner by ourselves." A week rarely passed when the couple was not visited by acquaintances, relatives, or strangers stopping by to pay their respects. Most visits required at least one meal to be served, and in many instances the visitors spent the night. In November 1799, for example, the last full month of Washington's life, the staff at Mount Vernon served meals and provided accommodations to outsiders on seventeen of the thirty days, and for five of those thirty, the former president was away from home.

In early November, he spent those five days surveying his property in a neighboring county and assessing another plot of land that he was considering taking in payment for some rent owed to him. While out, he journeyed across the Potomac to the District of Columbia, where he inspected a house that he was having built on a lot near the new Capitol building. He returned home on November 10 and resumed work on the plantation.

By the time he finished his sparse breakfast on December 12, the thermometer hovered around freezing and brisk winds blew toward the northeast. He delayed his daily farm inspection until close to ten o'clock, but then, donning a heavy coat and hat, he mounted his favorite horse and departed to ride across his holdings. Soon after, a light snow began to fall, eventually turning to hail, then freezing rain.

When he returned from his rounds at three, Tobias Lear was alarmed that his employer was soaked to the skin. "The snow was hanging on his hair," Lear noted. "He came to dinner without changing his dress." In the late afternoon the two men answered correspondence and, by evening, Lear reported that Washington "appeared as well as usual."

On the following morning, Washington awoke with a sore throat but considered it a "trifling matter," Lear wrote, adding that the former president "took no measures to relieve it; for he was always averse to nursing himself for any slight complaint." By 1 P.M., the storm clouds had disappeared, leaving the unobstructed sun beaming upon the glistening white carpet of snow. Washington took the break in the weather to identity and mark a few trees that were to be removed from the front lawn.

In the evening, he sat in the parlor with Martha and Lear and read a few newspapers that had been recently delivered. "He was very cheerful and, when he met with anything which he thought diverting or interesting, he would read it aloud, as well as his hoarseness would permit," wrote his secretary. After having Lear relate some recent proceedings of the Virginia Assembly, Washington prepared for bed. At Lear's urging that he take something for his sore and hoarse throat, he scoffed, "You know I never take anything for a cold. Let it go as it came."

During the early-morning hours of December 14, Washington awakened Martha, complaining of a sore throat and difficulty breathing. She begged him to send for a servant, but he steadfastly refused. Finally, at dawn, when a maid came into the room to build a fire, he instructed her to inform Lear of his weakened condition, to send for a plantation overseer named Rawlins who was adept at bleeding, and to notify his friend and neighbor Dr. James Craik.

Bleeding, or "bloodletting," a process believed to drain "bad humors" from the human body, was an archaic yet still accepted medical practice much in vogue in America during the mid- and late eighteenth century and consisted of making a surgical incision in a vein and allowing prescribed amounts of blood to drain into a basin. The procedure was highly regarded and recommended by Benjamin Rush of Philadelphia, the former surgeon general of the Continental Army and a signer of the Declaration of Independence.

Lear prepared "a mixture of molasses, vinegar and butter," but when Washington tried to swallow the potion "he appeared to be distressed, convulsed and almost suffocated." The overseer Rawlins soon appeared, clearly tormented at being called to perform such a serious procedure upon his employer. "Don't be afraid," commanded the hoarse patient, later suggesting that the incision be made even larger to allow more blood to flow. Meantime, Martha sent for a second doctor and pleaded that the bleeding be stopped and, after about a pint of fluid had been drained, Washington allowed Rawlins to halt the procedure until Dr. Craik arrived.

Craik had his patient gargle a mixture of tea and vinegar, applied heated blister packs to his throat, and let more blood. "No effect was produced . . . and he [Washington] continued in the same state, unable to swallow anything," wrote the anguished doctor as he instructed servants to send for a third physician.

When Drs. Elisha Cullen Dick, from nearby Alexandria, and Gustavus Richard Brown, from Port Tobacco, Maryland, arrived in mid-afternoon, they examined the former president, then conferred with Dr. Craik.

Craik and Gustavus Brown agreed that Washington was suffering from quinsy, an acute inflammation of the tonsils which sometimes led to the formation of abscesses. Dick suggested that the illness was much more serious than mere tonsillitis; he diagnosed it as "a violent inflammation of the membranes of the throat, which it had almost closed, and which, if not immediately arrested, would result in death." While Craik and Brown wanted to continue the bleeding, Dick strongly disagreed, arguing that an immediate tracheotomy be performed to enable Washington to breathe.

The tracheotomy was not performed, however, and the patient was bled once again, further weakening him. At 4:30 P.M. Washington asked Martha to retrieve two wills from his desk. When she returned with the documents, he reviewed them and told her to keep only the latest version and to destroy the earlier one. A little later he called Lear to his side. "I find I am going," he said in a low murmur that the faithful secretary could barely hear. "My breath cannot last long. I believed from the first attack it would be fatal. Do you arrange and record all my late military letters and papers—arrange my accounts and settle my books, as you know more about them than anyone else." He asked Lear if there was anything to which he needed to attend, since there was little time left. He sat for a few moments by the fire but was so desperate for breath that he soon returned to bed. For periods of time Lear lay beside him so that he could better turn his employer's large body and, from time to time, raise him on his pillows.

In a frail voice Washington told his physicians, "I feel myself going. I thank you for your attention. You had better not take any more trouble about me; but let me go off quietly; I cannot last long," and urged them to allow him to die "without further interruption." To Lear, he called once more and whispered, "I am just going. Have me decently buried, and do not let my body be put into the vault in less than three days after I am dead. Do you understand me?" "Yes, sir," replied Lear. "'Tis well" were the last words that the master of Mount Vernon uttered.

Just before midnight on December 14, 1799, surrounded by Martha, Dr. Craik, Lear, and a few of his favorite servants, Washington felt for his feeble pulse. Before Craik could reach the bedside, the president's "hand fell from his wrist," recalled Lear. Martha, sitting near the foot of the bed, caught Lear's eye and asked, "Is he gone?" The secretary nodded.

For four days after his death Washington lay in state at Mount Vernon in a mahogany casket crafted in nearby Alexandria. A silver plate mounted on the coffin read:

General
GEORGE WASHINGTON
Departed this life on the 14th of December
1799, Aet. 68

On the eighteenth, while a sloop moored in the Potomac River fired cannons, local militia troops escorted the cortege as it proceeded from the mansion to the family vault, followed by Washington's favorite horse, draped with his master's saddle, pistols, and holsters. Seventy-one Masons, representing the Alexandria and District of Columbia lodges, along with family members, neighbors, and six honorary pallbearers, attended the brief funeral, officiated by the Reverend Thomas Davis. Martha, desolated by her husband's sudden and unexpected death, was too ill to attend the services and remained at the mansion with her granddaughter.

Congress, in session in Philadelphia when news of his death reached the city on the day of the funeral, immediately adjourned. On the twenty-sixth, the declared official day of mourning, Henry "Light-Horse Harry" Lee, Washington's longtime friend, delivered a memorial address in which he said that the former president would always be "first in war, first in peace, and first in the hearts of his countrymen." Americans everywhere grieved for their fallen leader, and during the next two months nearly 450 eulogies were delivered across the country in scores of towns and communities.

Alexander Hamilton, Washington's secretary of the treasury and one of his most trusted confidants, proclaimed, "Perhaps no man has equal cause with myself to deplore the loss. . . . He was an Aegis very essential to me. . . . My imagination is gloomy. My heart is sad." Thomas Jefferson, the former secretary of state and a frequent critic of the president, recalled years later, "He was indeed, in every sense of the words, a wise, a good and a great man," adding, "Never did nature and fortune combine more perfectly to make a man great, and to place him in the same constellation with whatever worthies have merited from man an everlasting remembrance."

"Possessed of power, possessed of an extensive influence, he never used it but for the benefit of his country," said Abigail Adams, wife of President John Adams. "If we look through the whole tenor of his life, history will not produce us a parallel," and she prophesied, "Simple truth is his best, his greatest eulogy. She alone can render his fame immortal." Her son, the future president John Quincy Adams, wrote, "He is now beyond the reach of all bad passions . . . and his character will remain to all ages a model of human virtue, untarnished with a single vice."

The editor of the *Virginia Gazette* wrote, "Still be the Voice of Mirth! Hushed be all Sounds of Joy! In silent sorrow, mourn, Columbia, mourn! If loss of worth unequaled here below, be cause of grief or cause of woe and grief unbounded, bides thee mourn, thy worthiest, noblest Son is no more—ILLUSTRIOUS WASHINGTON is dead!"

When news of Washington's death gradually made its way to Europe, Napoleon Bonaparte, first consul of France and the beneficiary of the French Revolution during which Washington adamantly maintained American neutrality years earlier, personally delivered a eulogy and ordered a ten-day requiem. Simultaneously, the British navy ordered its fleet to fly ships' flags at half-mast, and in London, the *Morning Chronicle* editorialized, "The whole range of history does not present to our view a character upon which we can dwell with such entire and unmixed admiration. The long life of General Washington is not stained by a single blot. . . . His fame, bounded by no country, will be confined to no age."

In a letter to a friend, written eleven months before he died,

Washington included a passage that could well have been his own epitaph: "[I] always walked on a straight line, and endeavoured as far as human frailties, and perhaps strong passions . . . to discharge the relative duties to [my] Maker and fellow-men, without seeking any indirect or left handed attempts to acquire popularity."

Epilogue

ithin weeks of Washington's death, plans were undertaken to memorialize him. John Marshall, a congressman from Richmond, Virginia, introduced legislation authorizing the construction in the Capitol of a marble mausoleum that would house the former president's remains. After years of debate, the crypt was finally completed and plans made to move the bodies of both George and Martha from their resting places at Mount Vernon to the new tomb in time for the 1832 centennial celebration of Washington's birth. The transfer never took place, however, since John Augustine Washington, the president's grandnephew who inherited the estate, refused, citing the president's desire, as expressed in his last will and testament, to be interred at Mount Vernon.

The following year, a private organization, the Washington National Monument Society, was organized with John Marshall, the long-serving chief justice of the United States Supreme

Court, as its president. A competition was held for the design of a memorial to "harmoniously blend durability, simplicity, and grandeur," the winner being Robert Mills, whose plan featured a "grand circular colonnaded building . . . 100 feet high, from which springs an obelisk shaft . . . making a total elevation of 600 feet." The cost was projected to total $1,250,000 and a campaign was immediately implemented to collect the funds from private donations. By 1836 only $28,000 had been raised, and another twelve years passed before President James K. Polk, on July 4, 1848, supervised the laying of the monument's cornerstone at a site less than a mile south of the White House. Martha Washington's grandson, George Washington Parke Custis, attended the ceremonies along with twenty thousand other spectators.

By 1854 the shaft pointed 152 feet skyward but stood dormant for another twenty-two years due to lack of funds. In 1876 the Monument Society called on Congress for financial backing and, two years later, the United States Army Corps of Engineers took over the project. Meanwhile, plans for the circular colonnaded building to surround the monument's base were scrapped, and the height of the obelisk progressively increased to 555 feet, $5\frac{1}{8}$ inches by December 6, 1884, when the capstone was set. On a frigid February day two and a half months later, President Chester A. Arthur, standing before a nearly frozen crowd, proclaimed, "I do now . . . in behalf of the people, receive this Monument . . . and declare it dedicated from this time forth to the immortal name and memory of George Washington."

By early 1858, while construction on the Washington Monument languished, the former president's great-great-nephew, John Washington, the owner of Mount Vernon, faced a financial dilemma. Years earlier, the plantation had ceased to be profitable, becoming somewhat of a burden to Washington, its soil exhausted and its residents continually plagued by tourists wanting to see where "the father of his country" had once lived. Numerous attempts to interest both federal and state governments to take over the estate and create a national monument were futile. Meanwhile, a Mount Vernon Ladies' Association of the Union had been organized by Ann Pamela Cunningham, a South Carolinian determined to rescue the mansion from ruin. The funds to purchase the mansion and two hundred acres were raised by April 6, 1858, when John Washington and the Ladies' Association signed the purchase agreement.

Washington's family vacated the premises in early 1860. Ann Cunningham returned to South Carolina for a brief visit but was stranded when, in April 1861, the guns at Fort Sumter fired the opening shots of the Civil War. Her personal secretary, Sarah Tracy, had been left in charge of Mount Vernon and, for the next four years, the young woman courageously kept the mansion intact despite frequent skirmishes and battles in the neighborhood. She finally approached General Winfield Scott, the commander of the Union army, pleading with him to spare Mount Vernon. "God bless the ladies," replied Scott, thus providing immunity to Miss Tracy and her mission for the duration of the war.

When Ann Cunningham returned in 1866, she guided the

Ladies' Association and its restoration of Mount Vernon for the next eight years before she retired, pleased that the mansion was saved for posterity. In her farewell speech she pleaded:

> Ladies, the home of Washington is in your charge. Let no irreverent hand change it; no vandal hands desecrate it with the fingers of progress . . . though we slay our forests, remove our dead, pull down our churches, remove from home to home . . . let them see that we know how to care for the home of our hero.

Washington was one of the few men in history to achieve legendary status in his own lifetime. Since his death over two hundred years ago, hundreds of books and tens of thousands of pages have been written in an effort to dissect and diagnose his life, psyche, philosophies, and contributions to America and the world. In 1957 historian Mary Wells Ashworth may have come closest to defining the "father of his country" when she wrote in the preface to Volume Seven of Douglas Southall Freeman's monumental *George Washington: A Biography:* "He does not need the mist of tradition to obscure or to flatter. The visionary who would have him preserved as a paragon is guilty of disservice to a character that begs no partial light, and the 'debunker' who seeks to dramatize a failing will find little to exploit in Washington's life."

Today, reminders of Washington are all about. Thirty-one states contain counties named in his honor, more than any other person or namesake. Seven of the states in which these counties are located were of the original thirteen colonies. Eleven of the counties to utilize his name did so during his lifetime. Washington, D.C., the state of Washington, Mount Washington in New Hampshire, and the George Washington National Forest and the George Washington Memorial Parkway in Virginia are also named in his honor. Two counties named Vernon, in Louisiana and Wisconsin, were named after Mount Vernon.

What can be said or written about George Washington that has not already been recorded? He was a man of humility, yet strong principle; a warrior who showed no quarter to his enemy, yet when the conflict was over, forgave and even pardoned; a statesman who, in retrospect, so understood and interpreted the workings of a democracy that, today, historians still marvel at his near perfect insight into problems that faced the young nation. Born British, he became thoroughly American, recognized by friend and foe alike as the guiding light for the colonies in their fight for independence, and later, of the United States as it began its difficult journey to world recognition and respect. He could have been referring to the present instead of 1798 when he wrote:

> To expect that all men should think alike . . . would be to look for a change in the order of nature; but at so dangerous a crisis as the present, when every thing dear to Independence is at stake, the well disposed . . . might, one would think, act more alike. . . . But I will unite with you in a fervent wish, and hope, that greater unanimity than

heretofore, will prevail . . . and that, the young men of the present day will not suffer the liberty for which their fore fathers fought, bled, and died . . . either by supineness, or divisions among themselves.

ACKNOWLEDGMENTS AND SOURCES

I am indebted to Dale L. Walker, the general editor for the American Heroes series, for his guidance and wise counsel, and to Natasha Panza at Forge Books for converting my manuscript into a book. My thanks also go to Candy Moulton, author of *Chief Joseph* in the series, for her longtime support of my writings. To Tom Doherty and Nat Sobel goes my appreciation for the opportunity to write this book.

Fortunately, I had no problem finding material on Washington. Outside of Jesus Christ, and possibly Adolf Hitler, he has likely had more books written about him than any other figure in world history. Obviously, I could not read—or even cursorily review—all of these titles, or even a small portion of them. The books I did use in my research, I found to be evenhanded, informative, and accurately written by authorities in their field.

The absolute beginning point for my research was the seven-volume series *George Washington: A Biography* by Douglas Southall

Freeman (Volume Seven was written by John A. Carroll and Mary W. Ashworth), published by Charles Scribners's Sons, 1948–57, closely followed by James Thomas Flexner's *Washington: The Indispensable Man* (Little, Brown, 1974). Since I drew heavily upon Washington's own letters and addresses, the readily available *George Washington: A Collection* (Liberty Fund, 1988) was most helpful, as was the two-volume *George Washington: A Biography in His Own Words*, edited by Ralph K. Andrist (Newsweek, 1972). For those who desire to review a more comprehensive collection of personal papers, refer to Donald Jackson's monumental six-volume series, *The Diaries of George Washington* (University Press of Virginia, 1976–79). An old, but still valuable, biography that was also helpful was W. E. Woodward's *George Washington: The Image and the Man* (Boni & Liveright, 1926).

Information about Washington's childhood is sketchy and fragmentary. Other than the passing information in some of the more popular biographies, the single source that I found most helpful regarding this phase of his life was a small pamphlet entitled "George Washington Birthplace National Monument," by J. Paul Hudson (United States National Park Service, 1956). For details of the event that launched his military career—the delivery of Lieutenant Governor Robert Dinwiddie's letter to the French commander—I relied on Washington's own *The Journal of Major George Washington* (The Colonial Williamsburg Foundation, 1959). The sufferings of the French and Indian War, including the trying ordeal at Fort Necessity and Braddock's "Wilderness War," are ably covered by Walter O'Meara in *Guns at the Forks* (Prentice-Hall, 1965). Source documents dealing with the French and Indian War period and the years leading up to the Revolution can be found in *The Annals of America,* Volume 2 (Encyclopaedia Britannica, 1968).

Revolutionary War literature is abundant and all of Washington's campaigns are well covered in Douglas S. Freeman's works. Other titles that were helpful were *Valley Forge: The Making of an Army* by Alfred Hoyt Bill (Harper & Brothers, 1952); *America's Wars and Military Excursions* by Edwin P. Hoyt (McGraw-Hill, 1987); and *Atlas of American Wars* by Richard Natkiel (Arch Cape Press, 1986). For more specific information about accoutrements, weaponry, and military operations, the reader is referred to *Armies of the American Revolution* by Ian V. Hogg and John H. Batchelor (Prentice-Hall, 1975).

For biographical data about Washington's associates during the Revolution and the early days of the Republic, the following titles were useful: *The Book of the Founding Fathers* by Vincent Wilson, Jr. (American History Research Associates, 1974); *Anchor of Liberty* by C. Fred Kleinknecht (The Supreme Council, 33° Ancient and Accepted Scottish Rite of Freemasonry, Southern Jurisdiction, 1987); and *Colonial Spirit of '76* by David C. Whitney (J. G. Ferguson, 1974). Wonderful pictorial material was found in John Grafton's *The American Revolution: A Picture Sourcebook* (Dover Publications, 1975), and *1776: The Adventure of the American Revolution Told with Pictures* by Irving Werstein (Cooper Square Publishers, 1976).

Washington's presidency is exhaustively covered by Freeman and Flexner. Particularly interesting information about his involvement in the creation of the District of Columbia, as well as the salvation of Mount Vernon after his death, was found in *Rider with Destiny: George Washington* by Lonnelle Aikman (Link Press, 1983). Other helpful titles were *George Washington: America's First President* by Peter R. Henriques (Eastern National Monuments Association, 2002), and *G. Washington: Man and Monument* by Frank Freidel and Lonnelle Aikman (Washington National Monument Association, 1965). Many source documents relating to issues Washington faced as president are reproduced in *Documents of American History,* edited by Henry Steele Commager (Appleton-Century-Crofts, 1958). Both of his inaugural addresses are reproduced in *Inaugural Addresses of the Presidents of the United States* (U. S. Government Printing Office, 1989) and all eight of his annual addresses to Congress, as well as his Farewell Address, are included in *George Washington: A Collection,* cited above.

Washington's retirement was brief, less than three years, but the period is well covered by Freeman, Flexner, and Andrist. One need go no further than *George Washington's Mount Vernon: At Home in Revolutionary America* by Robert F. Dalzell, Jr., and Lee Baldwin Dalzell (Oxford University Press, 1998) for a fine rendering of the evolution of Mount Vernon from a small, inconsequential farm to one of Virginia's leading plantations, as well as Washington's role as gentleman farmer. Henry Wiencek's *An Imperfect God: George Washington, His Slaves, and the Creation of America* (Farrar, Straus and Giroux, 2003) might be the final word on Washington's emotional inner battle over slave ownership and his long-running desire to free them.

Finally, I would be remiss if I did not add that the views and conclusions expressed in the present volume are mine, and that if error or misinterpretation has crept into the pages, it is my fault alone.

INDEX

GW means George Washington.

Adams, Abigail, 154, 215
Adams, John, 28, 66, 67, 72, 73, 149,
    175, 200–202, 204–6
Adams, John Quincy, 215
Adams, Sam, 67
Alexandria, Va., 30
Allegheny Mountains, 139, 188
Allen, Ethan, 73, 124
André, Major John, 117–18
Andrist, Ralph K., 90
Annapolis, Md., 127, 132, 165
    convention at, 145, 171
anti-Federalists, 18, 171. *See also*
    Democrats-Republicans
Appalachian Mountains, 64
Armstrong, James, 150
army. *See* Army, U.S.; British army;
    Continental Army; militia
Army, U.S., 156
Arnold, Benedict, 73, 81–82,
    117–18, 123–25, 191

Arthur, Chester A., 218
Articles of Confederation, 128,
    144–45, 171
Ashworth, Mary Wells, 220
Attorney General, 155
Augusta, Ga., 165, 166
Austria, 180

Baltimore, Md., 93
Battle of the Wilderness, 45–47
Belvoir plantation, 68
Berkeley, Norborne, 67
Bermuda, 78
Bill of Rights, 156, 169
blacks, population of, 162
Blair, John, 155
Bland, Richard, 69
bleeding (medical), 211
Blount, William, 188
Boorstin, Daniel, 17
"born with his clothes on," 19
Boston, Mass., 76–78, 80–84, 157,
    158

Boston, Mass (*continued*)
  siege of, 82–83
  capture, 84
Boston Massacre, 67
Boston Tea Party, 67–68
Bouquet, Henry, 51
Braddock, Edward, 42–46
Bradford, William, 191
Breed's Hill, battle of, 76, 82
Bridenbaugh, Carl, 58
British army
  battle style, 76
  Boston occupation, 80
  GW in, 42, 46
  leaves New York at end of War,
    132
  surrender at Yorktown, 122
British navy, 80–81, 83, 90, 115,
    121, 122, 184, 215
Brooklyn Heights, N.Y., 89–90
Brown, Gustavus Richard, 212
Buchanan, John, 173
Buchanan's Station, 173
Bunker Hill, 76
Burgoyne, John, 98, 101, 107
Burr, Aaron, 200

Cabinet, U.S., 154–55, 190
Cambridge, Mass., 158
Camden, S.C., battle of, 118
Canada, 81–82
canals, 139, 145, 193
capital, U.S.
  building of, 181–82
  location of, 161, 162, 165
  See also New York, N.Y.;
    Philadelphia
Carpenters' Company, 69
cash crops, 61, 63, 185
census, 162
certificates of indebtedness, 144
Chad's Ford, Pa., battle of, 99–100
Channing, Edward P., 19

Charleston, S.C., 115, 129, 165
Chastellux, marquis de, 136
Cherokee Indians, 172–73, 188, 195
cherry tree legend, 31–32
Chesapeake and Ohio Canal, 140
Chickasaw Indians, 195
child labor, 158
Chippewa Indians, 168
Civil War, and Mount Vernon, 219
Clendinen, George, 163–64
Clinton, George, 149, 153, 181
Clinton, Henry, 108, 109–11, 113,
    114–15, 116, 118, 120, 123
colonies, united to wage war, 144
Concord, Mass., 70
Congress, U.S., 144–45, 156, 165,
    214. *See also* Continental
    Congress
Connecticut, 114, 140, 150, 157, 159
Constitution
  amendments to, 156
  approved and ratified (1787–88),
    148, 159
  on elections, 149, 150
  expressed vs. implied powers of,
    171
Constitutional Convention, 140,
    145–48
Continental Army, 73–75, 89, 130
  enlistments, 78, 89, 96
  pay issue, 129–30, 132
  regular army urged by GW,
    89–90, 95, 106
  supplies, lack of, 78, 102
  training, 78, 105–7, 129
Continental Congress, 88, 89, 93,
    98, 100, 108, 113, 127–28, 132,
    144
  First, 68–69
  Second, 70, 72–75
Conway, Richard, 150
Conway, Thomas, 104
Conway Cabal, 105

Cornwallis, Charles, 97, 100, 118–23
Cowpens, S.C., battle of, 119
Craik, James, 26, 64, 211–13
Creek Indians, 172–73, 195
Crown Point, 73
Culpeper County, Va., 30
Cumberland, Md., 140
Cumberland Settlements, 164, 172, 187–88
Cunningham, Ann Pamela, 219–20
currency, 75
Cushing, William, 155, 177
Custis, Daniel Parke, 55, 85
Custis, Eleanor Calvert (John's wife), 70
Custis, Eleanor Parke "Nelly" (step-granddaughter), 136, 202
Custis, George Washington Parke (step-grandson), 136, 218
Custis, John Parke (step-son), 55, 61, 70–71, 75–76, 121, 126–27
Custis, Martha Parke (step-daughter), 55, 61, 70–71

Dagworthy, John, 48–49
Dandridge, Frances Jones, 85
Dandridge, John, 85
Davis, Thomas, 214
Declaration of Independence (July 1776), 88
  signing of, 88–89
Declaration of Rights (June 1776), 88
Delaware, 114, 165
Delaware Indians, 168
Delaware River, 93, 109
Democratic-Republicans, 171, 174, 177–80, 184, 189, 200
Dick, Elisha Cullen, 212
Dinwiddie, Robert, 35–36, 42, 49, 64
District of Columbia, 165, 181

electors, presidential, 149
Elizabeth Town Point, N.J., 152
England. *See* Great Britain
English, population in North America, 33
Epsewasson plantation, 60
Estaing, comte d', 112
European warfare, 47, 76, 107
Eutaw Springs, S.C., battle of, 120

Factory System, 194–95
Fairfax, George, 57, 68, 73
Fairfax, Sally, 57, 68
Fairfax, Lord Thomas, 29
Fairfax, William, 29
Fairfax County, Va., 21, 58, 74
Fairfield, Conn., 157
Fallen Timbers, battle of, 187
Farewell Address, 20, 195
Fauchet, Baron, 181
Fauntleroy, Elizabeth, 56–57
Fauquier, Francis, 53
federal-state issues, 135, 145, 160, 171
Federalist Papers, 171
Federalists, 160, 172, 174, 177–80, 184, 186, 189, 200
Ferry Farm plantation, 27–28
"First in war, first in peace, and first in the hearts of his countrymen" (Henry Lee), 18, 214
Flexner, James Thomas, 47, 108, 182
Florida, 192–93
Forbes, John, 50–51, 53–54
foreign alliances, 195
Forks of the Ohio, 35, 37, 51
Fort Carillon, 34
Fort Chambly, 81
Fort Cumberland, Md., 43–44
Fort Duquesne, 34, 35, 42, 43, 44, 48, 50, 51–52, 53, 138
Fort Frontenac, 52

Fort LeBoeuf, 34, 35
Fort Ligonier, 52
Fort Machault, 53
Fort Massac, 53
Fort Necessity, 38–41
Fort Niagara, 43
Fort Pitt, 35, 53, 64
Fort Presque Isle, 34
Fort St. Frédéric, 43
Fort St. Johns, 81
Fort Ticonderoga, 34, 73, 82, 124
Fort Washington (N.Y.), 92
Fort Washington (Ohio River), 164
Fort Wayne, Ind., 164
France
    alliance with U.S., 108, 112
    recognition of Revolutionary
        government by U.S., 180
    recognizes U.S., 107
    relations with, in 1790s, 178–81,
        204–6
    Revolution of 1789, 173–74, 178
    rivalry with Great Britain
        (1750s), 33
    war with Great Britain (1790s),
        179
Franklin, Benjamin, 18, 129
Fraunces Tavern, 132
Frederick County, Va., 58–59
Freeman, Douglas Southall, 18, 220
French
    population in North America, 33
    volunteers for American cause, 99
French and Indian War, 33–54, 64
    cost of, and taxation, 65
    strategy of, 43, 50
French army, 116
French navy, 112, 120, 121–23, 127
French West Indies, 183

Gage, Thomas, 69–70, 77, 81, 82
Gates, Horatio, 75, 101, 104–5,
    118–19, 125

Genêt, Edouard, "Citizen," 180–81
George II, king of England, 42
George III, king of England, 64, 81,
    125
Georgetown, Md., 162, 165
Georgia, 150, 165, 173
Germantown, Pa., battle of, 100–101
Gist, Christopher, 35, 37
Grasse, comte de, 120, 121, 123
Great Britain
    allegiance to, 88
    holdings in Mississippi valley,
        163–64
    honors paid to GW on his death,
        215
    independence from, 87–88
    peace negotiations (1781–83),
        128–29, 132
    relations with, in 1790s, 179,
        183–85, 190–93
    rivalry with France, 33
    special envoy to (1794), 184–85
    strength of, vs. U.S., 72–73
    threat from, after War, 135
    treaty with (1794), 189
    war with France, 179
Great Dismal Swamp, 63–64
Great Kanawha River, 64
Great Meadows, Pa., 37
Green Mountain Boys, 73, 124
Greene, Nathanael, 119–20, 126
guerrilla warfare, 47, 107
Guilford Courthouse, N.C., battle
    of, 120

Hamilton, Alexander, 149, 157, 184,
    185, 191, 194, 204, 205–6
    in cabinet, 155, 177–80, 182
    described, 170
    leaves cabinet, 190
    political views, 160–61, 169–72
    praise for GW, 214
Hancock, John, 83, 88, 91, 100, 150

Harlem Heights, N.Y., battle of, 92
Harmar, Josiah, 164, 165, 168
Harrison, Benjamin, 69, 112, 135, 139
Harrison, Robert Hanson, 150, 155
Harrison, William Henry, 196
Harvard College, 158
"Have I got such troops as these?" 92
Hawthorne, Nathaniel, 18–19
Henry, Patrick, 66, 69, 148
Hessians, 90, 95–96
House of Representatives, 150
Howe, Richard, 90
Howe, William, 80–81, 82–84, 89, 90–93, 95, 97, 98–99, 108, 109
Hudson River, 92
Hudson River valley, British strategy re, 98, 113, 116
Hunting Creek plantation, 27, 60
hunting laws, 195
Huntington, Samuel, 150

"[I] always walked on a straight line," 216
"I can read three or four pages," 28
"I cannot tell a lie," 17, 32
"I find I am going," 212
"I have grown not only gray but blind," 131
"I heard the bullets whistle," 40
"If this be treason" (Henry), 66
independence, U.S.
    party of, 87–88
    recognized by France, 107–8
Indian tribes
    British incitement of, 184
    in French-British wars, 33
    raids on settlers, 178, 193
    trade with, 194–95
    wars with, 163–64, 168, 172–73, 187–89
Intolerable Acts, 68
Iroquois Indians, 37, 195

jackasses, 137–38
Jackson, William, 157
James River, 139
Jamestown, Va., 140
Jay, John, 149, 155, 157, 184–85, 189
Jay Treaty, 190–93
Jefferson, Thomas, 20, 28, 161
    in 1796 election, 200–201
    in cabinet, 155, 177–81
    and Declaration of Independence, 88
    described, 170
    leaves cabinet, 182–83
    political views, 160, 169–72, 174
    praise for GW, 17, 214–15
    as president, 197–98
Jones, Joseph, 115
Jumonville, sieur de, 38, 40–41

Kentucky, 164, 169, 193
Kings Mountain, S.C., battle of, 118
Knox, Henry, 82, 132, 147, 155, 157, 190, 205–6

Lafayette, George Washington, 202
Lafayette, marquis de, 20, 117, 127, 165, 167
    arrival in GW's camp, 99
    campaigns, 100, 110–11, 120
    praise for GW, 18
Lake Champlain, 73, 124
land speculation, 30, 34
Lear, Tobias, 25, 143, 157, 162, 205, 208, 210–13
Lee, Charles, 73, 75, 76, 77, 78, 80, 104, 109, 110–11
Lee, Henry (Virginia governor), 176, 185, 186
Lee, Henry "Light-Horse Harry," 18, 26, 28, 214
Lee, Richard Henry, 69
Lee, William (servant), 208
Lexington, Mass., 70

Ligneris, sieur de, 51–53
Lincoln, Benjamin, 122, 150
Little Turtle, 164, 168, 187
Long Island, N.Y., 89
Loudon, earl of, 50
Louis XVI, king of France, 173–74, 178, 179
Louisiana, 181
Loyal Company, 34
loyalists/Tories, 84, 87, 98, 114, 118–19

Madison, James, 28
    as president, 198
Maine, 158
Marshall, John, 217
Maryland, 48, 114, 139, 141, 150, 165
Mason, George, 88
Masons, 153, 182, 214
Massachusetts, 49, 69–70, 72–74, 88, 141, 146, 150, 158
McHenry, James, 205–6
McMaster, John Bach, 19
mercenaries, 90
Miami Indians, 164, 168
Middlebrook, N.J., 111–12
militia
    clashes with British, 73
    federal use of, 185–86
    GW's criticism of, 49, 89, 91
Mills, Robert, 218
Milton, John, 150
Mississippi valley, 138, 170, 192–93
    British and Spanish in, 163–64
monarchy, proposed for U.S., 130
money, 75, 144
Monmouth, N.J., battle of, 111, 113
Monongahela River, 45
Monroe, James, 198–99
Montgomery, Richard, 81
Montreal, 50, 81
Morgan, Daniel, 119

Morris, Gouverneur, 112
Morris, Robert, 98, 147, 162
Morristown, N.J., 113–14
Mossum, John, 57
Mount Vernon, 21, 25, 28, 41, 48, 59–62
    GW's occasional visits to, 121, 162, 181, 190
    GW's retirements to, between duties, 133, 201, 202
    history of, 60
    management of, 136–38, 143, 178, 185, 194
    remodeling of and repairs to, 60–61, 68, 134, 202–3, 220
    restoration as national shrine, 219–20
    slaves at, 61–62, 136
    unprofitability of, 150, 219
    visitors to, 209, 219
    wartime threats to, 120, 219
Mount Vernon Ladies' Association, 219–20
mules, 137–38, 204
Murray, John, 68
mutinies, 114, 119, 131
"My breath cannot last long," 26, 212

Napoleon Bonaparte, 215
national debt, 144, 160–61
navies
    GW's opinion on, 127
    See also British navy; French navy
navigation, 145, 156
Nelson, Thomas, 113
neutrality, 179, 180
New Amsterdam, 140
New Bern, N.C., 165
New England, 81
    British strategy re, 98, 116
    GW's tour of, 157
New Hampshire, 158

New Haven, Conn., 157
New Jersey, 92, 93, 114
New Orleans, 138, 163, 192
New York, N.Y., 89–93, 113, 120, 132
    battle of, 91–93
    as capital, 152–53, 161
New York (state), 74, 81, 84, 114,
    126, 149, 150
Newburgh, N.Y., 127, 129
Newburgh Conspiracy, 131
Nickajack Indian village, 188
Nicola, Lewis, 130
nominations and appointments,
    155–56
North, Lord, 108, 128
North Carolina, 63, 149, 163, 164,
    165, 172
Northeast, GW's tour of, 157
northern colonies/states, 72–73
Northern Neck, 29
Northwest Territory, 163, 168, 170,
    184, 187, 189
Norwalk, Conn., 157

oath of office, 177
O'Hara, Charles, 122
Ohio Company, 30, 34
Ohio River valley, 33–34, 138–40,
    170
Ore, James, 188
Osgood, Samuel, 155
Ottawa Indians, 168

Paine, Tom, 18, 93, 108
Parkinson, Richard, 203–4
Patowmack Company, 139
peace talks (1781–83), 128–29, 132
Peale, Charles Willson, 152
Pendleton, Edmund, 69
Pennsylvania, 114, 147, 163, 185–86
Philadelphia, Pa., 69, 93, 99, 100,
    101, 108, 109, 127, 146, 166
    as capital, 161, 162

Pickering, Timothy, 190, 191, 192
Pinckney, Charles Cotesworth,
    205–6
Pinckney, Thomas, 193, 200
Pitt, William, the Elder, 50
Pittsburgh, Pa., 64, 138
planters, debts of, 62
Polk, James K., 218
population, 33, 162
Postmaster General, 155
Potomac River, 27, 139, 162
President, U.S., 196
    counting votes for, 150–51
presidential elections
    1788–89, 149–51
    1792, 174–75
    1796, 200–201
President's House
    District of Columbia, 181
    New York City, 153
Princeton, N.J., battle of, 19, 97, 165
prisoners of war, 77–78
Proclamation of Neutrality, 180
Provision Order (British), 183
Prussia, 180
Putnam, Israel, 75, 77, 78, 80

Quartering Act, 65
Quebec, 50, 81–82, 124

Randolph, Edmund, 155, 183, 185,
    190, 191–92
Randolph, Peyton, 69
Rappahannock River, 27
Rawlins (overseer), 211
rebellions, 146, 185–86, 191, 201
Reign of Terror (France), 173
Residency Bill, 161
Revolutionary War
    beginning of, 73–75
    cost of, 112, 128, 143, 160
    end of hostilities, 131–32
    peace treaty, 132

Rhode Island, 78, 87, 149, 159
Richmond, Va., 165
Robertson, James, 188
Rochambeau, comte de, 116
Rockingham, Lord, 128
Ross, George E., 57
Royal Gift (jackass), 138
Running Water Indian village, 188
Rush, Benjamin, 211
Rutledge, John, 150, 155

St. Clair, Arthur, 165, 168, 187
Saint-Pierre, Legardeur de, 35–36
Saratoga, N.Y., battle of, 101, 107, 125
Sardinia, 180
Savannah, Ga., 115, 129, 165, 166
Schuyler, Philip John, 75, 76, 77, 81, 98
Scott, Winfield, 219
Senate, 150
settlers
    economic problems, 163–64
    forbidden to cross Appalachians, 64
    Indian raids on, 178, 193
Sharpe, Horatio, 48–49
Shawnee Indians, 168, 172–73
Shays, Daniel, and Shays' Rebellion, 146
Shenandoah Valley, 29
shipping
    seizure of, 183–84
    trade privileges, 189
Shirley, William, 49
slaves
    history of, in U.S., 140–42
    number of, 162
    provisions of GW's will re, 207–8
smallpox, 29
"something charming in the sound," 40
South Carolina, 126, 150, 165

southern colonies/states, 72, 74, 165–67
    British operations in, 114–15, 118–20
Southwest Territory, 187–88, 193
Spain
    boundary issues, 192–93
    gift from king of, 137
    and the Mississippi valley, 138, 163–64, 181
    treaty with (1795), 193
spies, 117
Springfield, Mass., 146
Stamp Act, 65–66
State Department, 154–55, 183
states
    conflict among, 145
    debts of, 161
    vs. federal power, 135, 145, 160, 171
Steuben, baron von, 106–7
Stony Point, 113
"summer soldier . . . sunshine patriot" (Paine), 93
Supreme Court, 155

tariffs, 156
taxation
    British, leading to War, 65–68
    U.S., after War, 144, 185
Taylor, Zachary, 196
Telfair, Edward, 150, 166
Tennessee, 164, 195
territorial issues, 163–64
Territories, 172. See also Northwest Territory; Southwest Territory
"These are the times that try men's souls" (Paine), 93
Thomson, Charles, 88
"'Tis well," 213
tobacco, 61, 63
Tories. See loyalists
Townshend Revenue Act, 65–66

Tracy, Sarah, 219
trade, 189, 194–95
Treasury Department, 155, 190
Trenton, N.J., 152
  battle of, 19, 95–96, 165
Trumbull, John, Jr., 126
Trumbull, Jonathan (b. 1740), 201
Turkey Foot, 187
Turtle Creek, 45
two-party system, 160, 195
Tyler, John, 196

United States
  discord in, 127–28
  planned increase in size (1798),
    205–6
  population of, 162
  problems of, 144–46

Valley Forge, Pa., 101–5
Vermont, 165
Vernon, Edward, 60
Verplank's Point, 113
veterans, 91, 127
Virginia, 63, 88, 139, 147, 148, 162,
    163, 165, 169
  House of Burgesses, 58–59, 63,
    66, 68
  landed gentry, 58–59
  militia, 31, 35, 36, 41, 48–49, 74
  presidents from (Virginia
    Dynasty), 196–99

Waldo, Albigence, 103–4
Walpole, Horace, 39
War Department, 155, 190
War of 1812, 188
Ward, Artemas, 73, 75, 77, 78, 80,
    84
warfare, European style of, 47, 76,
    107
Washington, Anne Fairfax (widow
    of Lawrence), 41, 60

Washington, Augustine (father), 27,
    60
Washington, Augustine (half-
    brother), 28, 30
Washington, George
  (1732) birth and boyhood, 27–29
  (1753) expeditions to west, 35–41
  (1754, 1758) resignations from
    military, 41, 54
  (1759) in Virginia House of
    Burgesses, 58–59
  (1759) marriage, 57–58
  (1775) chosen to command
    Continental Army, 74–75
  (1783) resigns commander's post,
    132–33
  (1787) attends Philadelphia
    convention, 146–48
  (1789) elected president, 149–51
  (1789) leaving retirement to
    assume presidency, 151–52
  (1792) attempts to reconcile
    Jefferson and Hamilton, 172
  (1792) stands for second term,
    174–75
  (1793) elected for second term,
    175
  (1793) inaugural address, 177
  (1796) decides to retire, 193–96
  (1796) Farewell Address, 20, 195
  (1796) last address to Congress,
    200
  (1797) final day as president, 201
  (1798) asked to assume command
    of armies, 204–6
  (1799) final illness and death,
    25–26, 209–13
  (1799) funeral and burial, 213–14
  agriculture practice, 21, 61–62,
    137
  animal husbandry practice, 137
  annual addresses to Congress, 163
  appearance and demeanour, 59

Washington, George (*continued*)
  biographers of, 18–20, 220
  burial place, 217
  commander of Continental Army,
    74–75, 95
  common sense of, 20
  critics of, 18, 104–5
  "deification" of, 17–18
  education, 28, 201
  eulogies on death of, 214–16
  financial problems, 62, 143–44,
    150
  General Orders issued by, 77, 88,
    129, 131
  health, 147, 154, 210
  historians on, 18–20, 220
  home life, 70–71
  important events during his
    administrations, 197
  journal, 151
  kingship proposed, 130
  land holdings of, 56, 63–64, 138,
    208
  last will and testament, 142,
    207–8, 212, 217
  legendary status of, 220
  legends about, 31–32
  letters, 66, 68, 73, 75, 91, 93,
    112–13, 114, 115, 135, 136,
    145, 149, 165, 167, 176, 184,
    191, 194, 201, 206, 216
  love life, 56–57
  a Mason, 182
  maxims compiled by as boy, 28
  memorialized in place names,
    220–21
  military opinions, 112, 114, 127,
    206
  military skill, 20–21
  as national hero, 19–20
  officer's rank, 36, 41, 48
  official tours of the U.S., 152,
    157–59, 165–67

as planter, 136–38, 194, 202
political views, 21, 66, 68, 73, 81,
  113, 115, 135, 145, 146, 148,
  155, 160, 172, 184, 221–22
praises of, 17–18, 214–16
as president, 153–56, 162,
  176–77, 201
as private citizen, 135–36
proclamation re loyalists, 98
reaction of country and world to
  death of, 214–16
retirements to Mount Vernon,
  21–22, 149
salaries declined by, 75, 150
slave holdings, 61–62, 136,
  141–42
social views, 158
surveyor work in West, 29–30
value of property at death, 208
in Virginia House of Burgesses,
  63
in Virginia militia, 31, 35, 36,
  48–49
Washington, George Augustine
  (nephew), 178
Washington, Jane Butler (father's
  first wife), 27
Washington, John (great-
  grandfather), 26
Washington, John (great-great-
  nephew), 219
Washington, John Augustine
  (brother), 76
Washington, John Augustine
  (grandnephew), 217
Washington, Lawrence
  (grandfather), 26–27
Washington, Lawrence (half-
  brother), 28–31, 57, 60
Washington, Lund (cousin), 120,
  134, 143
Washington, Martha Dandridge
  Custis (wife), 25, 55–56,

57–58, 70, 75–76, 85–86, 181, 211, 213, 214
character and appearance, 85–86
death, 86
as First Lady, 86, 153–54
provisions in GW's will, 207
visits to GW and troops, 85–86, 98, 127
Washington, Mary Ball (mother), 27, 29, 156
Washington family, 26–30
slave ownership of, 27, 140
Washington Monument, 218
Washington National Monument Society, 217–18
Wayne, Anthony, 113, 187
Weems, Mason Locke, 17, 22, 31–32
West Indies, 112, 190–91
West Point, N.Y., 116–18, 123
western frontier, 64, 168–69, 173, 178, 187–89, 193
Westmoreland County, Va., 27

Whiskey Rebellion, 185–86, 191, 201
White House plantation, 55–56
White Plains, N.Y., 92
Wilderness, battle of the, 45–47
Wilkinson, James, 104
Will (servant), see Lee, William
Wilmington, Delaware, 165
Wilson, James, 155
Wilson, Woodrow, 196
Winchester, Va., 49
winter quarters, 78, 97–98, 101–5, 111–12, 113–14, 127
Wolcott, Oliver, Jr., 190, 191
Woodward, W. E., 19

Yale College, 158
yellow fever, 181
York, Pa., 100
Yorktown, Va., 120
battle of, 121–23, 126

Ziegler's Station, 173

James A. Crutchfield is the author of forty books on aspects of United States history, including eight titles in the popular States of America series, plus *Tragedy at Taos: The Revolt of 1847, Eyewitness to American History*, and *Mountain Men of the American West*. His contributions to newspapers, magazines, and journals number in the hundreds. He has received the Spur Award and the Stirrup Award from Western Writers of America and is a two-time award recipient from the American Association for State and Local History. He presently serves as executive-director of Western Writers of America and resides in Tennessee with his wife, Regena.